THE ART OF ALLOWING

In memory of my brothers
Anthony and Louis

Louis Hughes OP

The Art of Allowing

THE BREATH IN MEDITATION AND IN LIFE

Illustrated by Anne Alcock

THE COLUMBA PRESS

First published in 2010 by
the columba press
55A Spruce Avenue, Stillorgan Industrial Park,
Blackrock, Co Dublin

Cover by Bill Bolger
Illustrated by Anne Alcock
Origination by The Columba Press
Printed in Ireland by ColourBooks Ltd, Dublin

ISBN 978 1 85607 694-4

Contents

Acknowledgements

A number of authors have inspired me through their insights into specific aspects of the breath. Dennis Lewis' *Free Your Breath, Free Your Life* (Boston, 2004) helped me become more aware of the effects of tension and bad posture. This book has many other wonderful exercises that I thoroughly recommend – for example: breathing into various parts of the body, belly breathing and the use of sound. Andy Caponigro's *The Miracle of the Breath* (Novato, CA, 2005) has too many wonderful features to mention here, but I would single out the Tarzan exercise, as well as those on strengthening the breath and the healing triangle. For more about the breath in yoga, you cannot do better than Rudra Shivananda's excellent *Breathe Like Your Life Depends On It* (Union City, CA, 2003).

All Scripture quotations are taken from the New Revised Standard Version, copyright 1989, by the Division of Christian Education of the National Council of the Churches of Christ in the United States of America.

I am grateful to the many people who have come on my courses over the years, and who continue to come. They have spurred me on to the extra effort of getting this material into print.

Finally, my particular thanks to Anne Alcock for her detailed line-drawings and to Laurence Freeman OSB for his encouraging Preface to this book.

Preface

St Anthony of the Desert once called his fellow monks to him from their cells in the desert. When they were gathered around him he gave them his teaching: 'Always breathe Christ.'

It was a short sermon but it says a lot and it is a good key to understanding the significance of Fr Hughes' new book on breathing. No doubt St Anthony was influenced by what was to become known, centuries later, as the hesychastic prayer of the heart of the eastern tradition of the church. No doubt it was already part of the practice of the first masters of prayer, including John Cassian, who opened John Main to this tradition in our time.

Resting the mantra on the wheel of the breath but giving the full attention to listening to the word, was John Main's advice. Like the desert teachers whose tradition he passed on, he did not write much about technique in meditation. Working with individual students or small groups, he would usually say more about posture and breathing as necessary. The important thing, though, is to keep it simple, to be faithful to it and, in time, to drop one's very self-consciousness about doing it. In time the meditator comes to appreciate another seminal saying by St Anthony: 'The monk who knows that he is praying is not truly praying. The monk who does not know he is praying is truly praying.'

Simplicity, practice and lack of self-conscious striving are the contemplative disposition to spiritual exercise. The modern mind that slips so easily into reductionism and focuses on technology rather than meaning can also easily trip itself up on this issue. Instead of putting these essential elements of the spiritual path to work, it gets hooked on techniques and quick results. Too much focus on technique can keep us in an arrested state of development.

On the other hand – and this is where Fr Hughes is a very

valuable guide for the modern spiritual seeker – we must not forget the body. One of the weaknesses of Christian spirituality as it developed in the last few centuries was the neglect of the physical dimension of our spiritual journey. Incredible as it seems for a religion based on the incarnation, believing that God took a body that breathed and felt like ours, prayer became over-identified with mental prayer or devotion. The heart was reduced to a squidgy emotional symbol and its meaning as an integrated centre of the whole human person was forgotten.

Preparing for contemplative prayer should be mindful and so should involve the body – by stretching, attention to posture or, as we see wisely and comprehensively described by Fr Hughes, by breathing. When the 'work' of meditation itself begins, consciousness then moves towards the total simplicity of, (for example) saying the mantra with full attention.

We breathe about thirty thousand times a day. To be attentive to a few cycles of respiration before meditation can remind us – as no words can – that to meditate is to lay aside thoughts and that this is really possible. As we face the complex issues of the planetary family today the simplicity and clarity that belong to wisdom are indispensable. Meditation as a way of wisdom – and how we prepare for it – has social as well as strictly spiritual significance. We need to hear this message of silence increase in volume in our time but then the silence itself needs to deepen. No wonder St. Anthony's sermon was so short.

Laurence Freeman OSB

Introduction

Breathing is not something that we ever need to do – we need only allow it to happen inside us. The breath is never 'my breath' – it does not belong to us. It is in some way greater than us, and it brings us life. This is a conviction that has slowly grown on me through almost forty years of practising body prayer and meditation. My journey began in 1971 when I joined the staff of St Charles' Seminary, Nagpur in India. While teaching there, I began the practice of yoga, and over time integrated selected physical exercises and meditation techniques into my own prayer and Christian meditation.

Since returning to Ireland in 1978 I have been sharing my experience with others through workshops and retreats. There were also a number of publications, notably the book *Body-Mind Meditation*, which came out in 1990. The seeds of the present work can be seen in it, particularly in its second chapter on the breath. Since then, the centrality of the breath has loomed ever larger for me, not just in what I teach, but in every aspect of my life. The present work highlights the breath as the starting point of rest and of every form of activity, its role in meditation and healing, as well as in letting go of old life and embracing the new. The book's core lies in its 46 guided breathing exercises. These are the accumulated results of reflection, meditative practice and sharing with individuals and groups over many years. They will reveal their value more and more through repetition.

Breathing meditation brings diverse benefits. It will help you to relax and to sleep better. It will also help you cope better with stress and tiredness. Through it you will learn to pray in more holistic ways; you will move towards your spiritual centre and become more open to God's call to friendship and intimacy.

You can work your way through this book, chapter by chapter or exercise by exercise – that would be the ideal approach. However, there are alternatives – expecially for busy people.

You can leaf through and stop at any point and have a go at any exercise that appeals to you. You do not have to work in any particular order (though in a few instances you will be referred back or forward for some details). Alternately, you can use the Chapters and Table of Exercises to go straight to whatever you like. Select and use what you can do most easily or what best suits your need at the moment. Do not feel that you have to 'cover' everything. Indeed, if you can find even one exercise that you feel at home with, you will have made good use of this book.

CHAPTER ONE

Allowing

 gave up breathing about twenty years ago. That is, I stopped thinking of breathing as something I needed to do in order to survive. The simple truth that came to me then is that there is nothing I needed to do about the breath – except relax and allow myself to be breathed. Let's think about this! Did you need to breathe when you were asleep last night? What steps did you take to ensure that you continued breathing from the time you woke up this morning up to the present moment? Have you been checking up on how the breath is working now even as you read this page? More generally, how do infants know how to breathe? The truth is that breathing is not something *we need to do* at all. Rather, breathing *happens* in us. It isn't so much that you are, right now, breathing – but rather *you are being breathed*. All you need do where breath is concerned, is to let go, relax and allow yourself to be breathed. There is really nothing at all to be done except receive the gift of the breath. This is a very simple truth and yet many of us have great difficulty taking it on board.

Almost from our first gasp at birth, we have been told, shown and taught how to breathe better: 'Breathe out!', 'Take a deep breath!', 'Inhale! – exhale!' There are innumerable sources of instruction on how to breathe 'correctly'. These include classes in yoga breathing (*pranayama*), Zen Buddhist belly breathing, various holistic and therapeutic breathing practices – in addition to books, audio-visual material and, increasingly, websites. These have a lot going for them, but many of them miss the fundamental point: natural breathing is not something that we actually need to learn – or that we even need to do.

It is very liberating to bring awareness to the breath and to discover that you don't have to control it. The aim to this chap-

ter is to help you experience the freedom of allowing yourself to
be breathed. The whole process of breathing is not something
that you own or that you are responsible for. It is purely a gift,
given to you each moment, in every cycle of breath.

Breath Control and Life Control
The Brazilian writer Paolo Coelho was arrested and brutally in-
terrogated by the Brazilian military dictatorship in 1974. Many
years later, he recalled the trauma he underwent at that time. He
commented: 'Remember how I thought that I was in total control of my life? Since then, never again have I felt in control. And
I'm glad. It was a most important lesson. You don't control anything, sir. You can be the most successful author, and then you
cross the street and you're dead. Tragedy can wait for you
around any corner. So now I take every day as a miracle. All my
books are factored by *carpe diem*, seize the day, because nothing
can guarantee you are going to see another sunrise. Only when I
understood that did I gain the strength to move on.'[1]

Wanting to be 'in control' is very much part of our contem-
porary culture. Coelho warns us here that our 'control' can in
the end turn out to be illusory. Of course it is important that we
take responsibility for our life and that we have some influence
over it. Many people live their lives in the shadow of another
person. Some have been mind-controlled or have suffered psychological abuse in a cultist or group situation. Others are co-
dependent. In these situations, a necessary part of the healing
process is learning to think for oneself and taking some charge
over one's life. We all need to work for our personal independ-
ence as we grow and mature. However, we can try too hard. We
can forget that at the deepest level we are not ultimately in control of our life, whether in its beginning, its ending or in the
space between.

Perhaps the greatest difficulty with allowing ourselves to 'be
breathed' is this strong urge to be in control. For some of us, as
for Coelho, learning to accept that we are not in control may
only come about through a deep personal crisis. But we don't
have to wait until we reach that point. We can learn to look at
the wonder and beauty of the world and of our own lives in a

1. From an interview in the *Sunday Times* (Magazine), 10/2/2002.

non-controlling way, without having to feel the need to improve or exploit these. On a visit to the Grand Canyon some years back, I noticed a man wearing a T-shirt. The logo was revealing: 'Came – Saw It – Bagged It'. Many people have difficulty with simply gazing and contemplating the beauty that is all round them, even something as wonderful as the Grand Canyon. Our outlook can be more economic than contemplative. The contemplative views a great forest as a place of mystery. An economist might see it in terms of the price per cubic metre that one might get for its timber.

Where the breath is concerned, the language we use already implies that we believe we control 'our' breath. We speak of 'inhaling' and 'exhaling', or 'breathing in' and 'breathing out'. When distressed, we are advised: 'Don't forget your breathing' or 'Breathe deeply', in order to keep calm. I can clearly remember as a teenager being subjected to some rather deep drilling to a tooth, and without anaesthetic. Before each touch of the drill, the dentist urged me to 'breathe deeply'. This may indeed be the most practical thing to do in tough situations. It may be hard to trust that you will be breathed. In the words of one woman who has had plenty of suffering in her life: 'It just won't happen. When under stress you have to actively breathe.' However, I believe we can all learn how to let ourselves be breathed, even in crisis situations.

Turning all your attention to the breath can be an invaluable resource when faced with sudden anxiety. Some years ago, I was trekking through an uninhabited jungle in the highlands of central India. I had left the trail in search of a spectacular viewing point that I believed to be near at hand. I lost my way and eventually woke up to the fact that I was lost. No viewpoint, not the slightest trace of a track anywhere in sight – only the silence of the trees and the dead leaves underfoot. I started to panic but fortunately I then remembered the breath. I stood still and, closing my eyes, drew my attention inwards. I became aware of speeded-up breathing, and also of the thumping in my chest. Focusing totally on the breath, I could hear it carrying my familiar prayer-word. Within a short time, my fear had passed, the breathing had slowed down and my heart was again ticking gently. The prayer-word had now quietened to a comforting murmur. And, no longer being in a state of panic, it dawned on me that, by facing back in the direction I had come, I could re-trace my steps through the trackless carpet of leaves. This I did carefully and after about twenty metres could just make out the faint line of the leaf-strewn path by which I had come.

When we realise that there is no need to organise or take care of the breath, but that it is the breath that takes care of us, we may be able to let go of our controls and simply allow ourselves to be breathed at the tempo that is most natural.

The breath – Not my breath
By developing a contemplative, rather than an economic approach to life, we learn to just look and be affected by the beauty of so many ordinary things round about us. Here the breath can be a great teacher. The reader will have noticed that I say 'the breath' rather than 'your breath' or 'my breath'. This is because the breath is not our private property. The more you practise awareness of the breath, the more you will come to realise that it is mysterious and yet very consoling. It is bigger than us and beyond us. We depend on it for our life, but it does not depend on us. And it is given to us, not just when we were born, but at every subsequent moment in our life.

Each time the breath enters our body through the nostrils, we are receiving a priceless gift. Like all gifts we should not grab at it – but accept it with appreciation and gratitude. We receive the gift not when we want it, but as the Giver offers it to us. As the breath leaves the body, we neither blow it out nor prevent it from leaving. We let it all go in its own time, and at its own tempo. We trust that the One who gave us the current breath will also give us the next one. Learning to look at, and above all to allow ourselves to experience, breathing in this passive way brings us to a realisation that our life, and particularly the present moment of it, is an awesome mystery. Who you are is so much more than the curious calculating ego that all the time demands to be in charge of the show.

Learn from children and animals

One community to which I belonged had a pet cat. It wasn't the sharp-eyed fleet-footed type, but a massive black and white neutered male. Dinky was everybody's pet, about as peaceful and inactive a creature as you could find. Most of his daylight hours were spent curled up on a couch in the hall. As he slept, the regular movement of feline lungs would from time to time produce a contented sigh. Occasionally, if I had to comfort a stressed visitor, the first thing I did was invite him or her to sit for a few moments and just watch Dinky – if they liked cats, that is! Usually it was a much less stressed individual who sat down with me a short time later. Dinky knew all about relaxation – as do most animals.

Children up to about the age of five have one special thing in common with animals – they are masters in the art of natural breathing. Without being taught by anyone, they allow themselves to be breathed, and have been breathed in this natural way from the first moments after they were born. Quietly sitting and watching an infant sleeping is instructive as well as relaxing. It can teach us how to let go and allow the breath to flow naturally. What is striking is how free the awakened child also is from inhibitions, and how its belly expands to the full with each in-breath. Without a socially acquired self-consciousness, the breath flows freely, naturally and fully. If we could only receive the breath as children do! The words of Jesus: 'Unless you change and become like children, you will never enter the kingdom of heaven' (Matthew 18.3) take on a new meaning when read in the context of breath. Some who have quietly watched a child sleeping, in reality or in their imagination while meditating, have been helped to recognise how much they tried to control the breath. One woman told me: 'The image of my sleeping child helped put me in touch with the more trusting child-like part of myself.'

All of us were breathed naturally throughout our earliest years, but possibly it didn't last. As over time children develop the capacity to reflect on the world round about them, they begin to make choices and unconsciously adopt attitudes that have a knock-on effect on their pattern of breathing. We are all shaped by the culture in which we grew up. This certainly was my own youthful experience. I grew up in an Irish town more than half-a-century ago. It was a macho society. Like every other young male I was expected to fight my corner from the age of seven or eight. I can recall sticking out my chest and putting up my guard like the boxers whose photos we saw in the newspapers or occasionally in the cinema. I learnt to strut about with my chest stuck out duck-like much of the time. Anything less was to show oneself up as a 'cissie'. Our culture then and now prizes chest expansion in men. In my youth body-building courses were widely advertised. The emphasis was on a rigid 'dynamic tension' of the chest muscles rather than on the fluid in and out movement associated with natural breathing. Over time such a posture can lead to a situation where men find it difficult to relax their chest muscles and allow the breath to move freely in that area. Young girls growing up in the same culture may have learned a parallel lesson: the waist was to be as narrow as possible at all times. 'Keep your tummy in!' was the message. This thinking over time has a restrictive effect on abdominal breathing. A tummy that expands and fills with air does not seem to fit in with the desired image of a slim, trim waistline.

Recovering Natural Breathing

Re-discovering the early experience we had of natural breathing involves a degree of unlearning. Above all, however, it involves trust and a willingness to be less controlling – and this applies not just to the physiological breath. It will embrace many of the adult life issues that we have taken on and made part of our-selves as we grew into and through adulthood. Our psychology and our spiritual values will be brought into play. The following pages in this chapter will describe a number of simple exercises which you can do on your own. These will focus on relaxing and becoming aware both of your body and of the breath. You can look on these as basic steps on the way to preparing yourself for more relaxed, natural and deeper breathing.

In doing these exercises it is recommended that you wear loose comfortable clothing. Remove your watch, glasses, jew-ellery and anything else that restricts the breathing or prevents you relaxing. The exercises are best performed lying down on a soft but firm surface. A carpeted floor, with a rug or sleeping bag, would be ideal. If possible try to do without a pillow. However, people with back, neck or knee problems may need one or more pillows or cushions – or may prefer to do the exer-cises seated. The most important thing is that your position be comfortable.

EXERCISE 1

Allowing the breath

1. Lie flat on the floor, arms by your side and with your feet slightly apart. The mouth should be lightly closed. Relax, close your eyes and become aware of the breathing.

2. Think of the air coming in and going out through your nostrils, but do not try to control it. Surrender to the smooth flow of air. Note the cool sensation in your nostrils as the air goes in; and the warm sensation as it goes out. Observe how the different parts of your body respond to the breath. First, think of your abdomen; next, the rib cage; and finally, the top of your chest. Take note of any movement, any expansion that might be occurring in your stomach, ribs or chest. Do not hold in your stomach or abdomen. Neither should you force them out. This is an occasion for letting go of all muscular control and letting things happen. Remember: you are not so much breathing as being breathed. There should be no effort of any kind.

3. Understand that full breathing is not something that you can earn or take by force. It is given freely to those who can receive it. Just allow the breath to flow freely, rather than try to dominate it. If you can simply relax and let go, you will find that the breathing, left to itself, will gradually slow down, deepen and become calm. With each in-breath God is giving you a priceless gift: life. Do not grab it or hold on to it – just accept it, receive it thankfully, and allow it to be.

4. At some point you may notice that, as the breath flows in, you have come to a 'tipping point'. You may be struck by the realisation that your body is more full of air than before. This is quite normal. If it seems strange or even frightening at first, that may simply be because of the novelty of the experience. Or you may have been unconsciously grappling with the fact that the breath is moving in a way that no longer conforms to some long-held idea about how you are 'supposed to' breathe.

5. Take some time to enjoy your new freedom to be breathed fully, and the sense of peace that comes with it. You may be surprised at how relaxed, light – even weightless – you may feel after ten to fifteen minutes.

It is important that you approach this exercise without any expectations, particularly concerning the 'tipping point' described above. Whether you reach it or not is not the important thing. Whatever happens or does not happen as you lie there is absolutely fine. Accepting things in this spirit will in time bring you to a point where you become more sensitive to the movement of the breath into and out of your body. As you learn to relax more and more, natural breathing will begin to develop within you spontaneously. This is the way you were breathed from the day you were born up to the time when dress, behaviour and cultural factors brought forced and unnatural breathing in their wake.

The three-way breath

When the breath is flowing freely and naturally, it goes into three broadly defined areas of the body. One can talk about different kinds of breathing associated with each of these areas:

1. *Low breathing*. This takes place when the abdomen moves in and out. As it moves out the diaphragm moves down, thus drawing air into the lower part of the lungs. Because of this, it is sometimes called 'abdominal breathing' or 'diaphragmic breathing'.

2. *Middle breathing*. Here the lower ribs expand outwards to the sides rather like on old-fashioned bellows. It is also called 'intercostal breathing', literally 'breathing within the ribs'.

3. *High breathing*. Also known as 'clavicular breathing' or 'collarbone breathing', this involves a small rising and falling at the top of the chest. This form of breathing has a very low capacity compared to middle and especially low breathing

It would be wrong to think of the three types of breathing as being totally separate from one another. While one of the three may dominate, it is rare that the other two are completely absent. When relaxed natural breathing becomes well established in a person, all three zones will become fully active. However, this complete breathing can only come about over time, and as a gift. You should never 'decide to do' breathing in the three areas. The pace must not be forced.

The following is an exercise to help you open up and allow the breath to move in the three zones.

EXERCISE 2

Low, middle and high breathing

1. Lying flat on the floor, rest both hands on your tummy with the two middle fingers touching at the navel. Relax completely, keeping your awareness on the point where the two middle fingers join. Then do nothing! Become as passive as possible, neither making anything happen nor stopping anything from happening. Make a mental note of any movement or lack of movement at the navel.

2. Bring your hands up and place the palms on both sides of the rib cage, with the fingers flowing over the lower rib on either side. There will now be a gap between the two hands. Again relax and do nothing. Simply observe what may or may not happen, on no account intervening to make anything happen or to prevent anything from happening.

3. Place your hands on the top of your chest. Rest the tips of the three middle fingers of both hands just below the collarbone on either side. Again relax completely, taking note of any movement.

The three stages in this exercise correspond to low, middle and high breathing.

If you noticed an up and down movement taking place at the navel, that was low breathing. It circulates more air than do the other forms of breathing. This is because the lower part of the lungs has a greater capacity than the upper parts. The up and down movement of the diaphragm involved in such breathing also causes an internal massaging of several abdominal organs.

A sideways expansion and contraction of the ribs and chest indicates that you were enjoying middle breathing, activating the middle part of the lungs.

An up and down movement at the top of the chest reflects high breathing, because it engages the upper part of the lungs.

While doing this exercise you may find yourself becoming anxious if you do not notice any movement either in the lower or middle part of the lungs. In fact some people don't seem to find movement in any of the three areas. That of course does not mean that they have stopped breathing! It is just that they have not yet learned how to become fully aware of the flow of the breath. Irrespective of what may or may not seem to be happening, the most important thing in this exercise is to relax, be passive and not worry.

Relaxation the Key

Relaxation is the key to natural breathing. This means relaxing not just your body, but also your mind and spirit.

The following series of exercises involves physical and mental relaxation, centring or focusing the mind, and a meditation on the love of God. You can do the exercises at different times or ideally as one continuous process. It is best to do them lying on a rug or sleeping bag, rather than in bed. Unless you are using the series to help you sleep, your bed may be just a little too soft to allow your body to lie quite straight and to rest naturally. If you have difficulty lying down at all, then simply sit comfortably. Do, however, try to keep your back straight, with your head well out of the shoulders. It is important that the room be warm, because when you relax deeply, your body temperature tends to drop. Before you begin, remove shoes, glasses, watch and heavy jewellery. Take plenty of time with each numbered stage, making sure that you are completely rested before moving on to the next one.

EXERCISE 3

Deep physical relaxation

1. Lie on your back on the floor, arms a bit apart from your sides, your feet about ten to fifteen inches apart. Check that your body is in a straight line, not curving to right or left.

2. Stretch your heels along the floor away from your body, your toes towards you – and relax. Expand the fingers of both hands to form stars – stretch and relax. Slowly roll your head from side to side a few times, leaving it in the most restful position.

3. Become aware of the weight of your body, and the points of contact between your body and the floor. Imagine that your body is very heavy, as if made of lead, pressing down into the floor. Next, imagine that your body is very light, like a feather, ready to float away. Finally, become aware of your body just as it is.

4. Take a few moments to become aware of the rhythm of the breath, noting how fast or how slow it is, and also where the breath is going to and coming from in your body.

5. Bring your attention to your left arm. Slowly raise the entire arm about an inch off the floor. Hold it there for a few seconds, feeling its weight. Then, as slowly as you can, lower your arm to the ground and relax. Next turn your attention to the right arm, raising and lowering it in the same slow, conscious way. Apply in turn the sequence of awareness-raising-holding-lowering-relaxing to your left leg ..., right leg ..., head and neck.

6. Rest for a few moments. Are you sufficiently warm? If not, then put something over you. If you find lying on your back uncomfortable, then lie on your front. Feel free to make minor adjustments to your clothing and position as you prepare to move on to a deeper level of physical relaxation.

7. Once more bring your attention to your left arm. Without raising the arm, gradually increase the tension in the muscles, slowly building up to a maximum. Consciously hold the tension for a few seconds. Then, as slowly as you can, ease back on the tension, releasing slowly and relaxing the arm completely. Repeat this procedure for your right arm..., left leg..., right leg...,

and neck. The sequence this time round is: awareness-tensing-holding-releasing-relaxing.

8. Become aware of the main areas of your body, checking for hidden tension. Survey your lower abdomen, stomach, chest, heart, throat, behind the eyes, shoulders and your back. Wherever you discover tension, slowly increase it, bringing it to a maximum, holding it there for a moment; and then slowly easing back on the tension, releasing and relaxing.

9. Continue this process until your body is deeply relaxed.

You can continue on from here seamlessly to the next exercise, which focuses on the mind rather than the body. However, feel free to conclude at this point or to at least enjoy a break before continuing.

EXERCISE 4

Mental relaxation and centring

1. As you lie relaxed on the floor, become aware of your thoughts. If you find yourself preoccupied by some anxiety or concern, do not try to push it away from your mind. Instead, gaze on it calmly.

2. Do not analyse it or try to solve any problem. Simply be aware of it there. Hold the distracting thought at arm's length for some time, not letting it slip away. When you are ready, release it, relax and allow it to float away. If it doesn't float away, you may need to hold it there a little longer. If another distraction takes its place, then you can deal with it in the same way.

3. Continue with the above process as many times as you like before moving on to the next phase – centring the mind.

4. Picture in your imagination a square, directly in front of you. It can be any colour and made of any material whatever. Inside the square there is a circle, the circle being slightly smaller than the square and not touching it. Inside the circle there is an equilateral triangle, smaller than the circle and not touching it. Let your mind rest on the figure of the square, containing the circle, containing the triangle.

5. Slowly move towards the figure, observing it grow larger as you approach it. Now veer to one side until you are just outside one side of the square.

6. Study the side of the square closely. What colour is it? What is it made out of? Mentally put your hand out and touch it. Note what it feels like.

7. Slowly pass in through the side of the square, so that you are inside the square, but outside the circle, and rest there. Turn your attention next to the circle, noting what it is like to look at and to touch. Pass through into the circle, remaining outside the triangle and pause there. Finally, go through the same procedure with the triangle, passing through one of its sides right into the centre of the figure.

8. Relax completely within the triangle. Enjoy being physically and mentally relaxed. Feel yourself protected by the triangle, circle and square.

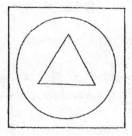

You may now like to take your meditation a step further. There is an even deeper level of relaxation which you can receive at the core of your spirit. Relaxation here depends on the conviction that you are supported by a loving, powerful Being. This gives you the freedom to let go, to trust completely, knowing that some One is supporting and taking care of you. The next exercise is designed to help you become more receptive to this dimension of God's unconditional love for you personally. You can read the triangle with its three sides as a symbol of the Trinity – one God but three Persons: the Father, the Son and the Holy Spirit. Within the triangle you can hear the words of Jesus as expressing that love for you at this moment – the aim of the next exercise.

EXERCISE 5

Infinite and unconditional Love

1. As you remain deeply relaxed in body and mind, and centred within the triangle, take some time to absorb one or more of the following phrases:

Do not let your hearts be troubled. Believe in God, believe also in me. (John 14:1)

Know that I am in my Father and you in me, and I in you. (John 14:20)

Peace I leave with you; my peace I give to you. I do not give to you as the world gives. Do not let your hearts be troubled, and do not let them be afraid. (John 14:27)

Abide in me, as I abide in you. (John 15:4)

As the Father has loved me, so I have loved you; abide in my love. (John 15:9)

2. Whenever you want to conclude the exercise, move slowly away from the centre of the triangle. Pass slowly in turn out through the triangle, the circle and the square. Withdraw slowly from the figure, observing it becoming smaller, and eventually disappearing.

3. Become aware of the fact that you have been meditating. Become aware of your body, of how heavy and relaxed it feels. Take note of the breath, of how slow, smooth and deep it has become. Gently bring your session to a close.

It is important to do this meditation slowly. The more time you spend with each gospel verse the better. You can, of course, make your own selection of texts as you find appropriate, provided that these offer you a way of being with your God, receiving the divine love and resting in it. As one person put it: 'I felt a strength and peace in the triangle, and a feeling for the first time of God's unconditional love. I had known it in my head, but had never really believed it.'

A simple adaptation of Exercise 3, *Deep physical relaxation*, can help you if you have difficulty sleeping. Even if you find it easy to sleep, doing the exercise that follows will deepen your sleep and leave you more refreshed on waking.

EXERCISE 6

Breathing to sleep

1. After you have got into bed, relax on your back for a minute or two, your feet apart and your arms just a little bit away from your body. Become aware of the breath – of being breathed.

2. On an in-breath, slowly raise your left arm by about an inch. Match the upward movement of your arm to the time taken for the in-breath.

3. When your lungs have filled up, hold your arm in the 'up' position. Then, as the air begins to flow out, slowly lower your arm in time to the out-breath, and relax.

4. As the next in-breath begins, repeat this sequence with the right arm, raising and lowering it on the in- and out-breaths respectively.

5. Continue this process in turn with your left leg..., right leg..., and your head.

6. Return to your left arm. This time, instead of lifting the arm, slowly tense up the muscles of the arm as the breath is flowing in – and relax the tension as the breath is flowing out.

7. Do the same in turn with your right arm, both legs and your head.

8. Relax completely on your back, keeping your awareness on the breath until sleep comes.

9. As you lie there, you may like to imagine that the breath is slowly murmuring a short prayer word.

As you do this exercise, feel free to pause as long as you want between the different moves. In fact, resting for one or two breaths between stages may help you to relax more deeply.

Passive breathing and Spirituality

By doing the exercises in this chapter, you let go of your own efforts and become passive before (and within) God. As you focus on allowing yourself to be breathed in a conscious state, you are drawn into a new and richer rhythm of lung expansion and contraction. If the breathing had previously been habitually shallow, you may find yourself becoming alarmed by the sheer volume of air coming in. This soon passes. You will become more relaxed and centred and this can also help you to pray and meditate. The relaxed breath gently draws you inwards and away from distracting noises such as traffic in the street outside. You will find yourself becoming opened up not just in body and breath, but also in spirit. For some people the Exercise 1, *Allowing the breath*, is sufficient to bring them into a spiritual experience. As one person put it, shortly after doing this exercise: 'God is breathing me, holding me, keeping me, sustaining me, maintaining me, supporting me, allowing me, wanting me, loving me into being.' Being able to let go and allow the breath to flow in itself implies no little trust and indeed promotes trust. The breath and your whole life come to be seen and received as gifts from God. This opens you up to the possibility of a deep awareness of and relationship with God.

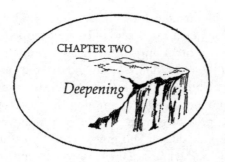

 arina came to see me because, as she put it, 'my breathing is very bad. How do I start to breathe properly?' She also told me she was asthmatic, hyper-active and prone to sudden panic attacks. As she sat opposite me I noticed that the breathing was rapid and concentrated at the top of her chest. There was little or no movement of the abdomen and lower rib-cage. I invited her to sit comfortably, and take time to become aware of her body and the breath. After about ten minutes of this, it was clear that the breathing was virtually unchanged. I then invited her to rest her hands, one on top of the other, on her stomach, and relax. After a few minutes of this, she became aware of a series of knots in her abdomen and stomach area. She also experienced a slight slowing down of the breath.

I then got Marina to place a gentle pressure on her stomach as the breath was going out, and to release the pressure as the breath was coming in. After about ten rounds of this, she arrived at some deepening of the breath. For her this was a breakthrough. She was discovering – or rather re-discovering – the experience of abdominal breathing. There was more. She spoke of what she was now experiencing: 'My mind was letting go of controlling my body and I felt pain afterwards in my rib cage as I felt many knots pulling from the neck to the spine and my rib cage.' Marina was becoming aware for the first time of many different sensations throughout her body. After a bit more of this practice she discovered some pleasant relaxing sensations in her back and elsewhere.

From doing these exercises, Marina was beginning to appreciate the connection between the tension and discomfort in her body and what was happening in her life. She was able to acknowledge that her shortness of breath was at least partly the result of living in her mind, and of being wrapped up in highly ambitious and at times unrealistic business projects.

Many people – like Marina – can find that they unconsciously resist 'being breathed'. They may be unable to become aware of the breath at all, even after attempting the exercises in the last chapter. The present chapter will offer a number of practical ways to stimulate deeper and more natural breathing. But first of all, we will look at some of the reasons why the breath may be unable to flow freely and fully.

Blocks to natural breathing

The most common reasons why breathing is restricted are bad posture and physical tension. Usually one is not aware of the affect these have on the breath. By becoming conscious of them you will easily be able to correct these restrictions. Before doing them, sit comfortably and become aware of the breath. Allow some time for the breath to become slow and relaxed.

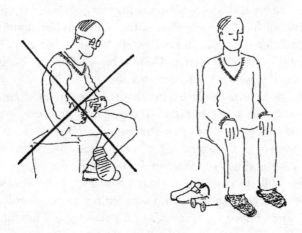

(1) Bad Posture

Here is a series of experiments to create awareness of the effects of three kinds of bad posture on breathing. Each of them restricts the movement of the breath in some way, and reduces breathing capacity.

EXERCISE 7

Slouching

1. Sit comfortably with your back upright and your head well out of your shoulders. Bring your awareness in turn into each of your legs, your hips, trunk, shoulders, arms until each part is relaxed and comfortable. Stretch your head around in different directions, bringing it to the place where it can rest nicely balanced without effort on your shoulders.

2. Become aware of the breath, allowing it to flow as freely as possible. Take note of how fast or slow it is, and which areas of your body it is flowing into and out of.

3. Lean forward as far as you find comfortable. Rest your arms on your thighs and allow your head to fall forward and down. Relax in this position as best you can and become aware of any changes in the way the breath is moving, compared to when you were upright. Continue in this slouching position for three or four rounds of breath.

4. Slowly straighten up. Sit upright and relaxed. Become aware of how the breath is now moving. Notice how it has become slower and deeper.

You will see how this exercise begins and ends in the natural, open posture where your back is straight and your body is relaxed. This helps to underline the effect of unnatural posture on the breathing.

EXERCISE 8

Leaning sideways

1. Sit upright and relaxed, bringing your attention to the breath as before.

2. Lean your head and your back over to your right side. Relax as best you can in the position. Become aware of where the breath is now moving. You will notice that it is almost entirely in the left side of your chest and abdomen. The right lung is scarcely involved at all.

3. Lean over on the left side, again taking note of the breath.

4. Sit up straight and enjoy the freedom of the breath flowing fully and freely into both sides of your body.

The next exercise involves what in my younger days was regarded as a lazy posture – leaning against a wall. Our teachers warned us to work hard at our lessons. Otherwise, our future might be 'keeping the wall up'. This was a local euphemism for idleness.

EXERCISE 9

Leaning against a wall

1. Stand upright near to a wall with your feet apart about the same distance as the width of your shoulders. Take a few moments to become nicely balanced and relaxed. Become aware of the breath and especially the parts of your body it is flowing into and out from.

2. Place your right shoulder against the wall and lean against it. Support your body with your left leg, allowing the right to go slack. As you bring your attention to the breathing, you will notice it is nearly all taking place in the left side of your body.

3. Repeat this exercise while leaning with your left shoulder to the wall.

4. Again stand in the upright position and become aware of the breathing.

It will be clear from these three exercises that sitting or standing upright, with your back straight and your head well out of the shoulders, is the correct posture for the best possible breathing. Each time you return to this posture, you will notice how much more easily the breath moves.

(2) Tension

To discover the effect of physical tension on breathing, stand at ease with your arms hanging by your sides. Your feet should be apart by about the same distance as the breadth of your shoulders. Take a few moments to allow your body to become nicely balanced between left and right foot, between toes and heels. Become aware of the movement of the breath.

EXERCISE 10

Tensing the body

1. After a few rounds of breathing, deliberately tense the muscles of both arms. As you hold the tension, take note of any tension building up in your body, and the effect that this has on the breath. After a few rounds relax your arms. Note how this eases the flow of breath. Enjoy this relaxed breathing for a few moments.

2. Tense both your legs. Again observe any tension that this creates elsewhere in your body. See how this too affects the breathing. After a while release the tension in your legs. Note how the breathing has become relaxed again.

3. Apply tension in turn to other parts of your body, for example: your abdominal muscles..., shoulders..., neck..., throat..., and face. Feel the particular effect that tensing each group of muscles has on the breathing. Relax each time after tensing and again feel the difference.

With practice you will see that tensing your arms, legs or abdomen restricts abdominal breathing. On the other hand tensing the shoulders, neck, throat or face causes a corresponding tension in the ribcage and chest – leading to a restriction of breathing in the middle and upper parts of the lungs. Generally speaking, tension in any part of your body will limit the movement of the breath. Many people habitually carry a great deal of unconscious tension in various parts of their bodies. As you experiment with these tensing exercises, you will find yourself becoming more aware of the particular ways that tension restricts the movement of the breath in you. One conclusion stands out: for the breath to move freely and fully, relaxation is essential.

Sitting with the breath

Generally, you can relax most deeply by lying on your back. However, for many breath awareness and meditation exercises, you will need to be relaxed while sitting. Perhaps when you first sit down your immediate preference is to sink into a heavily up-holstered armchair. While initially comfortable, this might mean that you will have to change your position from time to time. To sit still and relaxed for longer periods, the best option for most people is a firm upright chair. You are then ready for the next exercise.

EXERCISE 11

Relaxed sitting

1. Sit with your back straight, head well out of your shoulders. Lightly close your eyes and become aware of your body, how it feels at this moment. Become aware of the points of contact between your body and the seat, between your feet and the ground.

2. Become aware of the breath as it comes in and goes out. Take note of how fast or slow it is moving. However – and this is crucial – do not make the breath go fast or slow. Remind yourself that it is not so much that you are breathing, as that you are being breathed.

3. Bring your awareness into your left leg. Close your eyes and picture the leg. Try and get the 'feel' of your leg – what is your leg feeling just now? Are you aware of any tense muscles? Go on thinking about and sensing your left leg for a minute or two. It may help to imagine a small light shining on your leg. Gently move this 'light of awareness' up and down the leg all along its length from the hip right down to the toes. Within a very short time, you will notice the leg automatically beginning to relax.

4. Continue to move your awareness within your left leg, observing how it becomes progressively more relaxed. At some point, you may like to change the position of the leg, to make it more comfortable, so that it can relax even more.

5. Move your awareness from your left leg over to your right. Note how tense and unrelaxed the right leg feels compared with the left. Begin now to move your awareness within the right leg, just as you did with the left, until it too is completely relaxed and finds its most comfortable position.

6. Become aware of the soles of both feet. Slowly bring your awareness up through the soles and into the ankles. Continue up through the calves, knees, thighs, hips and on into the pelvic area – all the time noting a sense of relaxation following on awareness.

7. From the pelvic area move your awareness up through the lower back and abdomen; then the stomach and middle back;

and on to the upper back and chest, finishing up at the shoulders. Move across from one shoulder to the other a few times.

8. From the shoulders move down along the arms to the finger-tips, with both arms relaxing and finding their most comfortable positions.

9. Come back up through the arms and shoulders and on into the neck and throat. Gently move your head about, trying to find the position in the centre where it can rest nicely balanced without effort.

10. Again become aware of the breath. How slow or deep is it now compared with the beginning of this exercise?

What may surprise you as you do this exercise for the first time, is just how effective body awareness is as a means of relaxing. As you become aware of the different parts of your body, give particular attention and time to those parts that tend to become tense when you are under stress. Stay with each of these until they feel completely relaxed.

Stimulating the breath
There are simple and effective ways of enhancing the movement of the breath, and in a wholly natural way. In the exercises that follow, there is no direct intervention in the pattern of breathing – that is, you are not asked to 'inhale' or 'exhale'. You will still be breathed, rather than breathing, throughout each process.

The first exercise is designed to promote an expansion of the chest during breathing. It is named after the iconic film character, Tarzan. This exercise – practised by Tarzan – replicates the battle-cry of apes.

EXERCISE 12

Tarzan

1. Stand in a relaxed pose, checking that you are evenly balanced between your right and left feet, and between your toes and heels. With eyes closed, take a few moments to become aware of the movement of the breath. Take note of how fast or slow the breath is moving, and also of where the breath is coming to and going from in your body.

2. Follow the breath as it goes in, observing the pause between in- and out-breath. Then, immediately after the breath has begun to move out, produce a singing 'Aah' sound with your voice. At the same time start tapping your chest with the fingers of both hands, or with your lightly-closed fists. The tapping should be strong enough to cause staccato-like breaks in the sound, yet not so hard as to hurt.

3. Be sure to cease the tapping and singing before the out-breath is completed. Rest your arms by your side as you wait for the in-breath, before resuming the practice on the next out-breath. Continue for four or five rounds.

4. Pause, resting your arms by your sides. Take note of how different the breath is moving now, particularly in the chest area, compared with before the singing and tapping.

If you prefer, you can do Tarzan while sitting rather than standing. You can also vary the pitch of your singing in any way you like, if you prefer using 'Oh', 'Ee' or 'Oo' sounds instead of 'Aah'. Either way it will cause the breath to move more actively in your chest area. It will also help free up any blockages at the top of the chest.

Here is another exercise to promote chest breathing. It too can be done either standing or sitting.

EXERCISE 13

Breathing into back

1. Take a few moments to settle down and to bring your awareness to the breath, allowing time for its movement to become slow and relaxed.

2. Stretch both arms well out to the sides. Then, bring your out-stretched right arm round to the left and round behind your left shoulder. At the same time, bring your left arm round behind your right shoulder. If you can, hold on to your left shoulder blade with your right hand, and the right shoulder blade with your left. If this is too difficult, just hold on to the shoulders instead.

3. Holding this position, become aware of the breathing. Note how the breath seems to press out into your back. Continue for a few breath cycles, enjoying the sense of expansion in your back.

The following humming exercise is highly effective in promoting abdominal or 'low' breathing. It is particularly important that the sound and the breath be not forced in any way. Remember that you are not breathing – you are being breathed. And, just as the breath requires no effort, neither does the humming. It is simply a question of relaxing the breath and allowing it to flow in such a way that it seems to produce the sound quite naturally.

EXERCISE 14

Humming breath

1. Stand or sit upright in a relaxed and comfortable position. Bring your awareness to the breath for several rounds, taking note of its tempo and where it is going to and coming from.

2. Focus your attention on the out-breath. Just after it has begun to flow, and with your mouth closed, produce a resonant humming sound. Be sure to allow the sound to fade out before the breath has completely gone out.

3. Relax as you are being in-breathed. As soon as the breath has turned from 'in' to 'out', again produce the humming sound.

4. During the humming be aware of the vibrations in your forehead, sinuses, mouth and throat – and even in your ears and teeth.

5. After two or three rounds of the humming breath, again become silent, taking note of how much more easily the breath is now flowing in and out of the abdominal area.

Feel free to vary the pitch from one breath to the next and even within the same breath. You might also use sounds like 'Ah', 'Oh', 'Oo' or 'Ee' by opening your mouth on the out-breath. These other sounds are equally good for stimulating abdominal breathing. However, they will not produce the same degree of resonance in your head as does humming.

EXERCISE 15

Hands on stomach

1. Lie on your back or alternately sit back in an easy chair. Relax and allow yourself to be breathed.

2. Take a few moments to get in touch with the rhythm of the breath, taking note of the tempo and also where the breath is going to and coming from in your body.

3. Rub your hands together to warm them. Place one hand, palm facing down, on your tummy just at the navel. Then rest the other hand on top of it. Relax, keeping your awareness on your tummy where the hands are resting.

4. After a few rounds of breath, you may notice that the abdomen is rising and expanding more that it had been.

There are a number of variations you can make to this exercise. Instead of simply resting your hands on the tummy, you might instead:

(1) Gently massage round the navel with your fingertips.

(2) Tap your tummy, but not the navel, with your fingertips.

(3) As the breath is going out, gently press down into the tummy with your hands. But do not apply pressure until after the breath has started to go out. Be sure to cease pressing down before the out-breath is completed.

With practice you will discover which forms of exercise best suit you. Always allow rest time after an exercise, during which you can become aware of the effect it is having on how the breath flows in and out of your body.

Healing the breath

John is an elderly emphysema sufferer. This is the result of decades of heavy smoking which have left his lungs in a bad state. He is also prone to panic attacks and nervousness associated with a profound fear of dying alone. This has regularly led to his having to be rushed to hospital. He came to see me the morning after he had collapsed at a car-boot sale. He seemed in a bad way. Even slowly walking a hundred yards to my office left him completely breathless.

I gently guided John through the following breath-strengthening exercise. Less than half-an-hour later, he walked out into the street with his strength and confidence renewed.

EXERCISE 16

Breath strengthening

1. Sit comfortably with your back upright. Relax and become aware of being breathed. Remain focused on the breath for several rounds, allowing it to slow down. Take note of the tempo and depth of the breath.

2. Rest your hands on your thighs and form them into fists. Very gently and lightly tighten the fists. You will discover that the breath deepens and expands noticeably. Hold the tension gently and stay with the movement of the breath.

3. You may now gradually increase the pressure in your hands, though never to the point of causing pain. You will notice a corresponding degree of deepening and strengthening of the breath.

4. Begin to ease the pressure in your hands. Do this as slowly as you can. With some practice you will discover that even when the pressure has been completely released, the deeper level of breathing will continue.

The reason why this exercise is effective is that the effort of holding the fists tight makes additional demand for oxygen in the system. This stimulates deeper and stronger breathing. When doing this exercise for the first time, it is important that

you use only very gentle pressure initially. Don't try too hard! Otherwise you may create tension in other parts of your body and specifically in the chest and abdominal areas. And this would lead to a restriction and speeding up of breath – the opposite of what you want.

You can make this exercise easier by holding a pair of soft sponge balls in your hands. You can squeeze these instead of tightening your fists. These should be about the size of tennis balls, and in the shops are sometimes described as 'soft tennis balls'. Begin the exercise by sitting with your back upright, holding the balls gently in your hands as they rest on your thighs. Then continue as described in the exercise above. Using the sponge balls is particularly helpful if you suffer from arthritis in the finger joints.

The breath strengthening exercise can be very useful in coping with panic attacks. Moira was fearful of crowds. This led to her having to hastily withdraw from social gatherings. Typical was her comment: 'I did try to attend the celebration but when I arrived at the venue, within seconds I had a panic attack, so I left the hall and went home.' I asked Moira which type of meeting she would find most scary. She told me, 'A gathering of local people who know me for years and who would look on me as a failure.' I then invited her to sit quietly, become aware of her body and the breath. Within a few minutes she was nicely relaxed. I asked her to imagine that a large group of people who knew her well were gathered in the next room and she would be going in to meet them within a few minutes. This resulted in an immediate concentration of stress in her body, and a speeding up of the breath. I then asked her to tighten her fists so that the tension there matched the tension in her body. She continued to focus on the impending meeting, while at the same time maintaining the balance between the tension in her hands and the tension in her body. Gradually the tension eased and she became quite relaxed. The prospect of the meeting was no longer terrifying and she was now quite at ease about meeting the people concerned.[2]

In doing this exercise some people notice that the heartbeat as well as the breath gets stronger but not faster – that there was a correspondence between heartbeat and breath.

2. This practice is explained more fully in Chapter 5 and developed in Exercise 32, *The Healing triangle.*

Hand positions to promote breathing

The Indian yoga tradition uses hand positions (called *mudras*) to achieve calm, to rejuvenate the body and to promote mental well-being. Some of these automatically lead to a freeing up of the breath. The exercises that follow are particularly effective for improving your abdominal and chest breathing.

EXERCISE 17

Hand position for abdominal breathing

1. Sit comfortably with your back upright, head well out of the shoulders, your hands resting on your thighs, and with the palms facing upwards. Become aware of the breath, taking note of how fast or slow it is moving, and which parts of your body it is flowing into and out of.

2. Place the tip of each index finger against the side of the first joint of the corresponding thumb. Maintain a gentle contact between finger tip and thumb joint. Check that your body remains relaxed as you hold this hand position.

3. Bring your awareness back to the breathing. Within a minute or two, you should notice an expansion and deepening of the breath in the abdominal area.

It isn't necessary to hold the hand position for long. After four or five rounds of breath, you can gradually relax your hands. The deeper abdominal breathing which has emerged will usually continue by itself.

A different position for the fingers promotes intercostal or chest breathing by expanding the rib cage.

EXERCISE 18

Hand position for chest breathing

1. Sit quietly for some time, becoming aware of the breath pattern.

2. After some rounds, join the tip of the thumb and the index finger of each hand. For comfort you may curl up the other three fingers into the palm. Hold this position, while maintaining a gentle contact between thumb tips and finger tips.

3. Become aware of how this affects the breathing.

Some people have found that these hand positions freed them from the need to be in control of the breath. As one person put it, 'The positioning of my fingers drew my attention into my hands, and so, I let the breath go.'

Imagining the breath

The practice of simply following the inward and outward movement of the breath with one's mind is age-old. Some eastern spiritual traditions have developed it into an entire system of meditation. It leads to mental calming and centring of the attention and is an excellent remedy for psychological stress. The next exercise will introduce you to a simple yet comprehensive way of following the breath.

EXERCISE 19

Tracking the breath

1. Take a few moments to sit quietly, and become aware of your body. Bring your attention to the breath and stay with it for a few moments.

2. Focus on the inside of your nostrils. Note how the air, as it is going in, produces a cool sensation there – and a warm sensation as it is going out.

3. Now follow the in-breath as it passes through the nostrils and on down your throat, windpipe and into your lungs. Stay with this for several rounds of breath. Be aware of the stream of cool air flowing right down into your body.

4. Move next to the out-breath. Take note of the stream of warm air rising from your belly, passing up through your chest, windpipe, throat and nostrils.

5. Continue following the breath in this way for several more rounds.

If you have difficulty keeping your awareness on the breath as it passes through the different stages, why not use your imagination? 'See' the in-breath as a cool blue current coursing into your body; and the out-breath as a warm red current flowing out.

Breath freedom

The first conscious experience of 'being breathed' is a gift that may come to you when you least expect it. Think of the time when you first learnt to swim or ride a bicycle. After much splashing and sinking, balancing and falling, suddenly there was the moment of breakthrough – 'I'm staying up!' or, 'I'm not sinking!' That was an unforgettable moment of magic in your life. You did not take it by force. It came to you as a grace. A similar kind of breakthrough may happen while you are doing one of the exercises in this book. Or it can occur unexpectedly at some other time. One woman told me of how, during a breath retreat, she was sitting quietly on a garden bench. Suddenly she felt what seemed like a great torrent of air rush into her lungs. She thought her lungs were about to burst. The truth was that for the first time in many years she had let go and allowed herself to be breathed freely and fully. Others have reported that, as they became aware of the newly liberated breath, they immediately became fearful and tense. This led to the breathing becoming shallow and fast again. The reason for this is that it was many decades, way back in their childhood, since they had enjoyed natural breathing. When it suddenly re-emerged, it was quite unfamiliar and even seemed threatening. However, this sense of disorientation soon passed.

There is no need to be afraid of letting go and being breathed. Yet the rhythm of free, natural breathing may at first seem so strange that we feel an urge to change it. We may struggle to identify what is happening. It may seem as if the body is doing its own thing and we do not know what is going to happen next. This all reflects the difficulty we can have around peacefully observing what is going on without feeling the need to react. We may dread not being in control of the breath once we become conscious of it. Our uneasiness can in turn cause a speeding up of the breath.

There is however, a more fundamental reason for our unconscious reluctance to allow the breath. This is because becoming more aware of the breath brings us closer to all kinds of personal issues. We may find strong emotions such as anxiety, dread, anger or resentment coming to the surface. This points to a connection between the breath and what is going on in the deeper layers of our being. We will explore this theme in detail in the next chapter.

CHAPTER 3

Inspiration

ylvia, an elderly lady came to speak to me about her asthma. At least, that is what her doctor called it when she was with him some weeks before Christmas. Sylvia told me of her frequent experiences of terrifying breathlessness, accompanied by a sense of utter confusion. They were unstoppable and several times brought her almost to the point of passing out. Following that visit to her doctor, she was brought to hospital and spent Christmas there. This meant she was unable to discharge her usual routine of organising all the celebrations for her numerous adult family members.

I gently led Sylvia through a number of breath awareness exercises. Being attentive to the breath brought her to the realisation that the fundamental issue was not asthma, but her intense anxiety around the annual Christmas preparations. Her guiding principle had always been that 'it had to be perfect'. She was now beginning to understand that her insistence on doing everything to perfection was really a way of being in control, and that her unconscious efforts to control were wearing her down physically. For her, this insight was immensely freeing. Her breathing relaxed and deepened. She was now for the first time in many years able to be comfortable with something less than perfection.

One of the first things we notice about an upset person is the breathing. Faster, violent or irregular breathing indicates distress. On the other hand a relaxed, peaceful state is associated with breathing that is slow, deep and even. The connection between breath and spirit is very intimate. Observing the breath can tell so much about what is happening in a person's life. Whether laboured or calm, breathing is more than a physiological phenomenon. It is an expression of how a person is in mind, emotions and spirit at that moment.

As you begin to become more aware of your body and particularly of the breath, you are, like Sylvia, inevitably going to be brought face to face with issues in your life. That can sometimes take you by surprise, because our culture has taught us to unconsciously put distance between body and mind. This alienation from the body was well understood a hundred years ago. In *Dubliners*, his collection of short stories, James Joyce writes of one of his characters,: 'He lived at a little distance from his body, regarding his own acts with doubtful side-glances.'[3] However, this inclination to live away from one's body did not begin in Joyce's time. It can be traced back at least to the French philosopher, Descartes.

Our divided being

Descartes lived 300 years before Joyce. He was the mastermind behind analytic or co-ordinate geometry, familiar to students of mathematics. He was also a pioneer in many of the emerging sciences of the post-Renaissance era. However, he is best known for the founding principle of his philosophy: 'I think, therefore I am.' For Descartes, this is the most basic truth, and the one of which he could be most certain. He concluded that thought marks the true essence of the human person. This means that the body is not really essential to who I am. My body is not me – my mind is. With this step, Descartes' thinking parted company with the philosophers who had gone before. His dualistic way of looking at a human being was radically different from the holistic view that had prevailed in Europe up to that point. And its impact on today's world has been huge.

Descartes' thinking and later Enlightenment ideologies steadily eroded older philosophies of the human person. The new way of thinking gradually percolated down from an academic elite to affect every level of society. Today it influences how all of us in the western world, consciously or unconsciously, think and feel about ourselves. As in the case of Joyce's character, it can put a distance between the human person and his or

3. The character in question is Mr James Duffy of Chapelizod, in the story, *A Painful Case.*

her body. No longer do we see ourselves as a harmonious union of body, mind and spirit – living as part of a community in relationship with other people and the environment. The paradigm of the modern person is that of an individual ego-mind who inhabits and owns a machine-like body and who has a mission to analyse and exploit the world round about him.

Conventional medicine today strongly mirrors Descartes' divided understanding of the human person. Treatment has become increasingly technological. Complex, computerised instruments can now monitor every activity of each part of the body, sometimes even to the extent that a seriously ill person seems lost in a forest of electronic machinery, wires and tubes. Specialised medicine seems to treat a disease, a condition, a body part or an injury, rather than a person. It can fail to recognise the role that mind and spirit play in our health or lack of it. And its understanding of the breath is one-dimensional. The technical-medical perspective sees breathing as a purely physiological function, a mechanism for processing air as a form of fuel for the body. The notion that breath might be closely related to spirit is foreign to this way of thinking.

Happily, in recent decades, more and more people, including medical professionals, are starting to reflect critically on the mechanistic approach to health. The neurologist and neuroscientist, Antonio Damasio stresses the crucial role that emotions play in our rational thinking processes. He highlights the consequences for medicine of the split between mind and body: 'For the past three centuries, the aim of biological studies and of medicine has been the understanding of the physiology and pathology of the body proper. The mind was out, left largely as a concern for religion and philosophy, and even after it became the focus of a specific discipline, psychology, it did not begin to gain entry into biology and medicine until recently ... The result of all this has been an amputation of the concept of humanity with which medicine does its job.'[4]

You will find a fuller account of Descartes and his influence on today's culture in Appendix A.

---

4. Antonio Damasio, *Descartes' Error* (NY 1994), p 255.

Wisdom from the past

While an ego-centric perspective dominates today's culture in the West, older insights about who we are have not been entirely lost, particularly in regions that are less affected by modern civilisation. In large parts of the developing world, being part of an extended family and a local community is what counts. Most Africans, Asians and Latin Americans would pity the individual who was isolated from others. Their approach to life is beautifully captured in the African principle of *ubuntu*, which means: 'a person becomes a person through other people.'[5] A striking example of ubuntu in action was seen in the aftermath of the devastating earthquake that struck Haiti early in 2010. The *New York Times* wrote about a ten-year-old boy who 'ate only a single bean from the heavy plate of food he received recently from a Haitian civic group. He had to make it last. "My mother has 12 kids but a lot of them died," he said, covering his meal so he could carry it to his family. "There are six of us now and my mom." No matter what is found, or how hungry the forager, everything must be shared.'[6]

In the older cultures that preceded today's world, people did not make any distinction between breath and the human spirit. This is reflected in the fact that the great classical languages use one and the same word for both. This was the case over thousands of years and in widely different parts of the world. Sanskrit was the principal language of ancient India. It has one term, *prana*, which can be translated as 'breath', but equally well as 'life-force' or the spirit of a person. The equivalent term in Chinese is *chi* (as in *t'ai chi*). This same word is sometimes written as *qi* (as in *qigong* – pronounced '*chi kung*'). *Chi* (or *qi*) means both 'breath' and 'vital force'.

The same plurality of meaning is also found in the languages of the Bible. The Old Testament was written mainly in Hebrew. Here the term *ruach* can mean 'air', 'wind', or 'breath' – but also 'spirit'. The New Testament, written in Greek, uses *pneuma* with the same multiple meanings. The English words 'pneumonia' and 'pneumatic', with their associations with breath and air, are derived from *pneuma*.

---

5. As found in Albert Nolan, *Jesus Today – A Spirituality of Radical Freedom* (NY 2008), pp 15, 18.
6. *New York Times* online, 26 January 2010.

The consensus in all of these earlier cultures, which include the Judaeo-Christian world and its scriptures, is that breath is not something that exists and functions in isolation from the human spirit, the mind or any other part of us. It is an embodiment of what is deepest and innermost in us.

This connection between breath and spirit survives in folk memories even in the 'developed' West. Part of Sebastian Barry's novel, *The Secret Scripture*, is set in the northwest of Ireland during the civil war of the 1920s. A priest is called to minister to a young republican who had been shot by State forces: ' "Is he long dead?" said Fr Gaunt, "Did anyone take his last breath?" "I took it," said the brother. "Then give it back into his mouth," said Fr. Gaunt, "and I will bless him. And let his poor soul go up to heaven." So the brother kissed his dead brother's mouth, returning I think the last breath that he had taken at the moment of his brother's death. And Fr Gaunt blessed him and leaned into him, and gave the sign of the cross over him.'[7]

As you engage with the breath, you will find yourself becoming more sensitive to what is going on deep inside your mind, heart, emotions and unconscious.

If you would like to learn more about the terms used for 'breath' and 'spirit' in the languages of the Bible and in other ancient languages, see Appendix B.

Spirit, Breath and Wind

The various meanings of the Greek word *pneuma* are particularly striking in the third chapter of Saint John's gospel. Here Jesus is instructing Nicodemus, a leading member of the Pharisees, who had secretly become his follower. The message is that one can enter the kingdom of heaven only through being born again 'of water and Spirit' (John 3:5). Verse 8 has Jesus declaring: 'The wind blows wherever it chooses, and you hear the sound of it, but you do not know where it comes from or where it goes. So it is with everyone who is born of the Spirit.' The force of this line cannot be fully appreciated in English or in any modern language, where the words for 'wind' and 'spirit' are unrelated to each other. In gospel Greek, however, both are rendered by

---

7. Sebastian Barry, *The Secret Scripture*, (London 2008), pp 43-44.

pneuma. And with both, it is not possible to predict in what ways they will move.

The guided meditation that follows is based on the multiple meanings of *pneuma* in John 3. You can do it out of doors, when the weather is not too cold or wet. However, even if the weather is cold or stormy, you can do it while walking. Another option is to practise it sitting indoors with the window open. An ideal time would be a summer's evening which often brings up a pleasant breeze before sunset. Whatever time or place you choose, ensure that you have sufficient clothing or a rug to keep yourself warm. Begin by taking a few minutes to make yourself comfortable.

EXERCISE 20

Hit by the wind

1. Become aware of your body and the breath. Allow sufficient time for the breath to become slow and smooth.

2. Focus on your sense of hearing. Make a mental 'shopping list' of all the different sounds that you can hear – birdsong, dogs barking, children at play, work sounds, aircraft, music players, machinery, traffic etc.

3. Do not let yourself be annoyed with sounds that you might not like – for instance, loud music in the garden next door or the revving of an engine. Simply note each sound and then wait on the next, making no judgement for or against any one of them.

4. Allow the sounds to happen and do not strain to hear them. Relax and let each sound register on your consciousness.

5. Pay particular attention to any sounds connected with the wind – rustling of leaves or of anything else being moved by the wind. Hear the wind running through trees, hedgerows or shrubs.

6. Note how the wind rises in strength and suddenly fades away. Feel the way it gusts and changes direction without warning. Get a sense of the Lord's words: 'You do not know where it comes from or where it is goes.' Relax, flow with the sound, the force and the direction of the mysterious wind.

7. Become aware of the wind against your skin. How does it feel? Again note changes in direction and intensity. Receive the wind peacefully, irrespective of how it is behaving.

8. Focus in on the breath, allowing yourself to be breathed, to be filled by the wind, receiving what it is offering you, as a reminder that 'The wind/breath/spirit blows wherever it chooses.'

This exercise can help you experience in a concrete way the connection between wind, breath and spirit. It can lead you to feeling more alive and in communion with your body and the environment. In the words of one practitioner, 'My senses seemed to be more acute: lungs seemed to expand more, feeling of great hunger for *pneuma* – a sense of being filled in my whole being – then a sense of being one with the whole of creation – exhilaration felt with each breath.'

Breath and the Prayer of Surrender

By allowing yourself to be breathed freely and fully, you are saying with your body that you accept life whole-heartedly, that you embrace the circumstances of your life in this present moment. However, for many people this surrender may not be possible to begin with. Anxiety, fear or traumatic experience may have paralysed their spirit. This can lead to a distortion in the natural flow of breathing, making it tense, shallow or uneven. In this way the breath truly mirrors the condition of the soul. But there is also a positive aspect to the parallel movements of breath and spirit. By practising awareness and relaxation of the breath, you can over time find healing for your soul and a renewed faith.

In the gospel of Luke, just before his death on the cross, Jesus prayed the words of Psalm 31: 'Father, into your hands I commend my spirit' (Luke 23:46). Here Luke has Jesus using the word *pneuma*, which, as we have seen, can mean either 'spirit' or 'breath'. This means that the last prayer of Jesus can equally well be written in English: 'Father, into your hands I commend my breath'. As the gospel points out in the very next sentence, that is exactly what Jesus did: 'Having said this, he breathed his last.' Each one of us in our time will be called on to do just this in our final moments. In dying as in living, breath and spirit are inseparable.

The call to let go is, however, not just for the moment of death, but is there constantly through life. There are many things that we would be better off letting go of, yet somehow we still cling to them. These may include losses we have experienced but not fully accepted: of money, property, a family home, a career, a relationship – above all, a deceased loved one. There may be many less tangible attachments of which we may be more or less conscious: cherished projects, mental attitudes, hurts, resentments, judgements, jealousies, our self-image or anxiety around our own mortality.

The meditation that follows is an exercise in 'letting go' spirituality. Becoming aware of the breath and of the spontaneous tendency to control it has the potential to guide you to addressing the control issues in your life. That acknowledgement alone will be sufficient to weaken the hold that the particular issue has on you. Then, in the final part of the meditation, focusing on Jesus in his act of self-surrender can be a powerful inspiration in bringing you to the freedom that results from a fuller letting-go both of the issue and of the breath.

EXERCISE 21

Breath surrender

1. Lie flat on your back, with your feet apart and arms just a little bit away from your sides. Relax. Take some time to get in touch with the breath, giving it time to become slow and even. Observe the breath as it flows in and out of your body. How fast or slow is it moving? How shallow or deep? How jerky or smooth?

2. Call to mind the words of the prayer, 'Into your hands, Lord, I commend my spirit.' As you keep your awareness on the movement of the breath, imagine that the breath is gently murmuring these words. As the breath is going in, hear the phrase 'Into your hands, Lord' – and as the breath flows out, the phrase 'I commend my spirit.'

3. Allow the words to fit into or be moulded into the length of the in-breath and the out-breath. Do not in any way adjust the breathing to the words. 'Listen' as the breath whispers the prayer for you. Relax – allow yourself to be breathed and also allow yourself to be 'prayed through' in the breath. Continue with this breath prayer for five or six cycles of breath at least.

5. After some time focus your attention on the in-breath. As the breath comes in, be sure not to inhale or draw the air in. Simply relax and allow yourself to be filled. Do not take a breath. Instead receive the breath as a gift.

6. As your lungs fill up do not restrict the in-flow of air in any way. Allow yourself to be filled to the full extent that the breath is being given to you in this moment. Relax and accept the gift in its fullness.

7. Turn your attention to the out-breath. As the breath goes out, do not exhale or blow the air out. Just relax and let the breath go. As your lungs empty out, you may find yourself, consciously or unconsciously, not wanting to let all the air go. Some

little voice may be urging you to hold on to some of it – just in case the next breath does not come. Relax completely and let it all go, trusting that you will be looked after, really making your own the words 'I commend my spirit' – or more concretely 'I commend my breath.'

8. After practising this breath-prayer for some minutes, you may discover that some issue from your life comes into your consciousness. This will usually be something that has to do with letting go. You may find that this disturbs your meditation for a short time. The smooth slow rhythm of the breath may be hit by a period of turbulence. If this happens, simply focus all your awareness on the breath itself for at least a few rounds. You will discover that it will gradually slow down and resume its slow, even pace.

9. You may like to take this meditation a stage further by visualising Jesus on the cross praying these words: 'Into your hands, Lord, I commend my spirit.' Imagine the breath of Jesus moving exactly in time with the breath in you. With these words Jesus and you are now being breathed and being prayed through in unison.

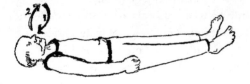

Practising this breath prayer can lead you to a deeper sense of yourself as really commending or committing yourself to God, trusting and putting yourself entirely in God's hands. Also, it connects your prayer with the prayer of Jesus. As you go deeper into this meditation you will gradually become more at one with Jesus as he prays to the Father.

Feedback

This meditation can be surprisingly relaxing. The releasing of the out-breath in particular expresses trust, and a willingness to let go. It invites you to let go of your concerns, to surrender your life without reserve to the God who gives it to you in the first place. The extent to which you are able to allow the out-breath to be free, reflects in some way your willingness to hand your life over to God. So much of your energy can be tied up in mentally holding on to what is unreal or at least no longer real in your life. This exercise can help you to become aware of this mental effort, and also to realise just how tense the muscles of your body, particularly those connected with breathing, have become as part of this holding-on process. When you let go of all tension, stress, thoughts and control – focusing simply on the rhythm of the breathing – the sense of relief, of having a burden lifted from your shoulders, can be palpable. You become physically relaxed as well as mentally centred, with your focus set on the breath.

Doing this exercise can also bring you to a profound sense of the unity of breath and spirit. It can feel as if your spirit is being breathed and renewed, leading to a greater awareness of a loving God in the deepest centre of your being. As one person put it: 'I felt breathed, and God's presence very close.' The process of letting the breathing just be, can become an expression of how life can be if you just trust that God is with you and that his thoughts for you can only be good.

Moving on to the visualisation stage of the meditation builds on all of the above. The image of Jesus can be of great help in letting go – particularly if you look on him in his greatest act of self-surrender. In the words of one meditator: 'You said to image Jesus breathing beside you … It was at that point that I felt surrender of my control. My heartbeat and breathing were in unison with Jesus' heartbeat and breathing. It was the closest I've ever felt to Jesus and a beautiful experience of love and peace.'

CHAPTER 4

Movement

 armel was 80 years old and had recently under-
gone heart surgery when she joined one of my
courses. She could walk only very short distances
and suffered from severe back pain. I noticed how
she shuffled around and remained close to the retreat centre
where we were staying. On our third day, I accompanied the
group through some exercises designed to co-ordinate physical
movement with breath rhythm. This included a simple exercise
of 'walking to the breath'. Later that day, Carmel started her
usual careful stroll. She took just one small step at a time, gently
keeping her awareness focused on the movement of the breath.
She continued like that and, to her amazement, she actually
found herself completing a substantial coastal walk without significant pain.

This incident reminded me of a scene in the film *Forrest Gump*.
Here, the main character, a young boy called Forrest, is scared of
the world around him. He has had severe problems with his
legs, which had to be supported by callipers. While travelling on
a school bus, he is bullied by other boys. In order to escape, he
flees from the bus, in his panic not noticing that the callipers
have burst open and fallen away. He discovers he can out-run
his pursuers. This amazing discovery is immensely liberating.
So, he just keeps on running until he is far from the town. He
continues running for days and weeks until eventually, he
reaches the west coast of the United States.

Now, virtually any activity that we engage in will be greatly
enhanced if it flows from an inner harmony. This is particularly
true if we work with, rather than against, the breath. A good
example of this harmony is the graceful movements of *t'ai chi*.
Somewhat more spectacular is the karate expert who splits a

solid piece of timber, or even a brick, with the side of his hand. This is no mere stunt but rather a demonstration of the power that results from bringing together breath, movement and intent. The power of the breath is real and exists, usually unrecognised, in each one of us. Anyone can use this gift, although in less dramatic ways than the last one mentioned above.

The breath is strong
If you would like to explore the relationship between breath and physical strength, the exercise that follows might be a good way to begin. It might also prove useful the next time you find yourself struggling with a hermetically sealed jar or bottle that just refuses to open.

EXERCISE 22

Screw-cap opening

1. Hold the container in one hand and the screw-cover in the other. Relax and close your eyes. Become aware of the breathing, giving it time to really slow down.
    2. Visualise the cover becoming loose and opening in your hand. Hold that image of movement in your mind and, as the breath begins to go out, apply as much force as appropriate to the jar and lid. The result may surprise you.

Some professionals such as nurses receive training in lifting patients safely and easily. The secret is working in teams and with the breath. I was once on the receiving end of this technique while fully conscious. It was for demonstration purposes only and I was the guinea pig. I lay on a table and five female nurses easily lifted me high into the air, using only one finger of each hand, i.e. ten fingers in all. This was possible because all five had synchronised the out-breath at the moment of lifting.

The next time you have to lift a suitcase, a chair or some other heavy object, do not rush into action. Instead try doing it like this:

EXERCISE 23

Easy lifting

1. Stand quietly before whatever you want to lift. Grip it lightly, bending your knees and your body for comfort. Then pause, relax and become aware of the breath – closing your eyes if this helps you to centre. Observe the in-breath and the out-breath for a round or two.

2. Wait for the out-breath to begin. Just after the breath begins to flow out, make your effort to raise the object.

It may help if you imagine that the breath is like the tide. As a sailor allows the ebb tide to carry his boat out to sea, so you simply allow the out-breath to carry the weight of what you are lifting. You may find that it seems to float up by itself.

This same approach can help you get over a fence or a gate when walking in the countryside. Before climbing just pause for a moment and allow the breath to slow down. When you are rested, place your hands on the top of the fence or gate. Wait for the breath to turn from in to out. Let your climbing movement follow in the wake of the out-breath.

This approach to physical activity is very different from

'mind over matter'. Here, we listen to the wisdom of the body and the breath, rather than the mind and its agendas of control.

The breath and walking
In his book *For a Pagan Song,* Jonny Bealby describes an epic journey on foot through the Hindu Kush mountains of Afghanistan and Pakistan. He is in search of an isolated tribe barely touched by the outside world, which until recent times had held on to ancient Hindu beliefs. However, their homeland is surrounded by jagged 5000 metre peaks. In the beginning Bealby found the going excruciating. He writes: 'We began to climb. Within seconds my feet felt like lumps of lead, my breath rasped in and out at a frightening rate and the smile of joy that had covered my face on the walk across the plain was replaced by a pitiful grimace. Everything I carried seemed to double, triple in weight …'[8] Fortunately he had a guide, John, who was able to teach him how to survive as a mountain walker: '"The secret to walking in the mountains," explained John, a few yards ahead, "is to get your heart, lungs and feet working in rhythm. If any one of them is out of sync, it's a bloody nightmare. Stick behind me, you'll be fine." Once I got the stride of my feet working in unison with my breathing, my heartbeat seemed to follow. I could feel the rhythm, all three vital parts working like a metronome.'[9]

You don't have to go to the Hindu Kush or the Alps to benefit from walking in harmony with the breath and the heartbeat. In fact, it will be easier to practise if you start by strolling gently on a smooth level path. Choose a quiet location – this can be indoors or out of doors – where you are less likely to be distracted, to try the next exercise.

8. John Bealby, *For a Pagan Song* (London, 1998), p 102.
9. Ibid., p 136.

Walking to the rhythm of the breath

1. Stand at ease, with the distance between your feet about the same as the width of your shoulders. Become aware of the rhythm of the breath, allowing yourself to be breathed.

2. Give yourself time to reach a relaxed meditative state – focusing all your attention on the breath. Allow yourself to be breathed.

3. After a while, you may sense that your body feels like moving. If so, just let it move any way at all – swaying, marking time, dancing, walking or whatever. Do not plan anything, do not do anything. Just don't stop your body from moving. Let it be free to move as it feels like!

4. If at this point you find that your body remains unmoved, then on an out-breath step down gently with your left foot, and on the in-breath step down with your right foot. Continue this stationary walk for five or six rounds.

5. Move your left foot just a little bit forward on an out-breath, and your right on the in-breath. After continuing this for some time, you may find yourself quite naturally doing two or more steps to each in-breath and each out-breath.

6. You can now begin to walk slowly and naturally while still keeping your awareness on the movement of the breath. Allow your feet to move by themselves. It might help to imagine that your feet are like two little puppies that you let out for a walk. Relax, let them out and allow yourself to be walked!

It is important not to try too hard at this exercise or to start working out in your head the ratio of steps to breath. As you walk, just take note of the number of steps as the breath goes in, and again as it goes out. In the beginning there will probably be one or two steps to each in-breath or out-breath. However, the number doesn't really matter, though it will probably increase as you gradually pick up speed. Do not force the breath or your steps in any way. The most important thing is to allow the breath to flow at whatever tempo it wants, and to let your steps fall in with this. And all the time keep your awareness within your body and on the breath. It goes without saying that, to engage properly in this, you will need to leave your ipod or discman at home.

As well as walking out-of-doors, you can also do this exercise on a walking machine. This has the advantage of allowing for a more constant relationship between breath and movement. Also, there may be fewer distractions.

Walking to the breath may seem a little complicated the first time you try it. In reality, provided you don't try too hard, it will emerge by itself in a wholly natural way. If by any chance you find yourself becoming tense or confused during this exercise, then forget about it for a while. Walk as you are accustomed to. After some time you can again gently bring your awareness back to the breath. Simply observe yourself being breathed and observe yourself walking. You may suddenly get the feeling that, rather than walking, you are being walked. To return to what was said earlier in connection with being breathed – do you remember the first time you learnt to swim or to stay upright on a bicycle? It came unexpectedly as a graced moment, and was quite unforced. Walking to the breath is like that. In the words of one person, 'I just focused on the breath and then the walking just happened'.

The breath's hidden resources

Jack Kyle, the Irish rugby legend, speaking as an 83 year old of his sporting achievements, said: 'When somebody says "How did you score that try?", all you can say is "I haven't a clue. A gap appeared", or "I got the ball and I started running and other gaps appeared and I got through them." I don't know how I did it. You're not working at a conscious level. You're at a low subconscious level where there is basic instinct or whatever it is. And there were times – and perhaps this is a very corny saying, but there's an element of truth in it – sometimes people say you weren't so much playing the game but that the game was being played through you.'[10]

10. From an interview with Shane Hegarty in the *Irish Times* 21/3/09, *Weekend Review*, p 7.

If you allow the breath to run freely, you too will discover that the game of life will be 'played through you', and that 'gaps' – even in the most stubborn of situations – will start opening up. You will discover resources of energy you never knew were there. Following the group practice of 'walking to the breath' on one of my retreats, a woman spoke of how she went for an afternoon snooze, and then, 'I wakened fully refreshed and feeling strangely light. Energy was simply there. Then, walking with a friend at what I thought was a leisurely pace, I was surprised when she turned at the end and said, "That was some pace you set." I was not even breathing hard. Where the energy came from I do not know, all I know is that the breath flowed easily and naturally'

Walking to the breath is energy efficient. It is how young children and animals walk and run. Unless we try to control our movements with our minds, our body will of itself tend to seek that which is most natural. If, over a few days, you practise walking with breath-awareness, you may well find that your walking pace will spontaneously match itself to the rhythm of the breath in a wholly natural way. One person, after doing this exercise, described it as 'effortless – as if my breath had taken me for a walk'.

Moving in this self-reflective way is more pleasurable and less tiring than the usual 'driven' way we have of getting about. It keeps us in the present moment. Even if this is about getting to work, or walking for health and fitness, you don't need to worry about how far you can walk, or have to walk. Simply allow yourself to be breathed and then it will feel as if you are being walked – so effortless will walking become.

Climbing the stairs, going uphill or walking faster than usual will cause your lungs to open up, naturally drawing in more oxygen per breath. You may also find yourself spontaneously taking shorter and fewer steps with each round of breathing. Then, as you reach level ground again or enter a downward slope, you may find the number of steps per breath increasing again. This is because you now need less oxygen per step, whereas your expanded lung movement continues to deliver at the higher rate needed while climbing.

After you have become comfortable with walking to the

breath, you may like to include awareness of your heartbeat. If you have difficulty in finding the heartbeat, then wait until after you have exerted yourself, for instance at the end of an uphill climb or after having lifted a heavy object. This exertion makes the heart work harder, at times even leading to a thumping sensation in the chest. Try then to stay with the hearbeat as it gradually slows down and becomes gentle again. What tends to happen is that, once the breath and movement are synchronised, the heart tends to adapt automatically. You will find heartbeat and breath synchronise naturally – as was Jonny Bealby's experience.

Bicycle breathing
Through what I call 'bicycle breathing', I discovered the bicycle as an aid to prayer, while on a cycling trip through quiet moorland in Co Cork. Working my way slowly uphill on that amazingly traffic-free road, the only sounds were the lowing of distant cattle, the song of an occasional bird, and the sighing movement of the ever-expanding breath as I worked the pedals. I was aware of that breath rhythm and let it lead me. It seemed to make the pedalling easier.

The key to bicycle breathing is matching your pedalling to the breath – the topic of the following exercise.

EXERCISE 25

Cycling to the breath

1. As you start your ride, take at least five or ten minutes to gently warm up. If possible head for quiet countryside or parkland – as flat as possible – where you will be free to give at least some of your attention to what is going on inside, as well as outside, of you.

2. Relax in the saddle as much as possible. Don't try too hard. Be content with a gentle cruising speed. Become aware of the breath, allowing yourself to be breathed.

3. Take note of how many rounds of pedalling you are doing to each in-breath and out-breath.

4. At the beginning of each out-breath and of each in-breath

apply downward pressure on a pedal. There may of course be several other pedal strokes in between.

5. Continue to allow yourself to be breathed and let the movement of your legs on the pedals flow naturally from the rhythm of the breath.

The joy of this practice is in the actual cycling itself, rather than the desire to reach a destination. It is not a question of effort, but of listening to the breath and to your body. You may even have the sense that, as well as being breathed, you are also 'being cycled'. The ups and downs of most roads will lead to some variation in the ratio of pedal strokes to breath. Going uphill you may find yourself taking as little as one stroke per breath. At other times, particularly going downhill there may be many pedal strokes to each breath and some of the time you will find yourself free-wheeling.

If cycling on the open road does not appeal to you, you can practise on an exercise bike at home or in the gym. The advantage here is that your pedalling can be more regular. Plus, you can close your eyes and focus all your attention on the breath and the movement of your legs on the pedals. Of course, you may not find the gym's background music helpful.

Movement and Meditation
You can make your walk, cycle-ride, use of a rowing machine, swim, and even climbing the stairs into a simple form of meditation by introducing a prayer word.[11] Become aware of the breath as you move along. Simply 'listen' to the breath and then imagine that the breath is murmuring or whispering any short prayer word or phrase. This should all be quite unforced.

When engaged in physical work, you might keep some of your awareness on the breath. This will help you work in a more fluid, harmonious way. If the breath speeds up, it may be telling you that you are pushing yourself too hard, like a constant companion who occasionally urges you to take things easy. Whenever you need to use greater force – pause, relax and get in touch with the flow of the breath. Then make your effort on the

---

11. There will be much more about prayer words in Chapter 7, Exercises 40 to 43.

out-breath. Staying with the breath will lead you gently towards the integration of work and prayer. In time, you may begin to 'hear' the breath echo a prayer word or short phrase even during heavy work. You will then be tuning into a centuries-old spirituality attributed to St Benedict. This is summed up in the Benedictine motto: 'To work and to pray' or perhaps, as some would rather read it: 'To work is to pray.'

Swimming is probably the exercise where we are most conscious of the breath. A happy swimmer knows the steady rhythm of breath in, breath out, spitting water occasionally. The learner knows the delight of moving from splashing around to staying afloat – to discovering that the water will support you. When you reach the stage of trusting the water and its buoyancy, your strokes move to a slower and more relaxed rhythm. And provided the water is not too cold or too rough, you can turn over, float on your back and relax. Then, looking up at the sky (or the ceiling of the leisure centre), the water will cradle you and allow you to be breathed. Whenever I have the opportunity to rest on the water in this way, I am reminded of the words of scripture: 'Cast all your anxiety on God, because he cares for you' (1 Peter 5:7).

Yoga and T'ai chi
Certain kinds of physical exercise not only lend themselves to becoming prayerful: they were developed specifically for a spiritual purpose. *T'ai chi* is sometimes called 'moving meditation', and its smooth flowing action follows the movement of the breath precisely. It attempts to tap into the *chi* or 'natural energy of the Universe', in order to heal any imbalance that may exist in the individual between the active (*yang*) and passive (*yin*) principles of the cosmos. This imbalance is believed to be the root cause of all mental and physical ill-health. However, apart from promoting good health, *t'ai chi* also leads naturally to a deep meditative stillness.

Yoga postures too are most beneficial when done in a manner that respects the natural rhythm of the breath. What that means in practice is that the effort of lifting or stretching is usually done on the out-breath. In most cases a stretched, folded or twisted bodily position can be held for a few cycles of breath. This has the effect of giving an internal massage to specific groups of vital organs, thereby stimulating and rejuvenating their activity. However, beyond the physical benefits, the postures have traditionally been seen as preparation for the sitting positions used in prolonged meditation.

For further information on the breath and yoga, see chapter 8.

Unlike yoga or *t'ai chi*, competitive sports may not immediately lead to centring. Rather, by their nature they tend to draw the spirit of the player outwards towards the objective of scoring or defending. However, as in the example of Jack Kyle given earlier, some of the greatest stars have been able to engage in sport in a centred, meditative way.

Breath, movement and prayer

The following group of exercises is an easy way to bring together breath, movement and prayer.

EXERCISE 26

Centred standing

1. Stand upright with your feet apart, back straight, toes pointing forward – the distance between your feet being about the same as the width of your shoulders. Let your arms hang by your sides and raise your head well out of your shoulders. Become aware of the breath, observing it as it becomes slow and even.

2. Without leaning over, bring your entire body over your right foot, so it bears almost all of your weight. After a few moments, bring the weight of your body likewise onto the left foot. Next, bring the weight into the centre so that you are evenly divided between right and left. In the same way bring your weight forward onto your toes, and then backwards onto your heels – being careful not to over-balance. Finally, bring your weight to the centre so that you are evenly balanced between toes and heels, between left and right.

3. Become aware of the contact between your feet and the ground. Slowly bring your awareness up through the soles of the feet, ankles, calves, knees, thighs, hips and into the pelvic area. Continue to bring the awareness upwards through your body as far as the shoulders. Let your arms hang freely as you bring your awareness down to the finger-tips. Note how your body relaxes as you do this.

4. Return to the shoulders, and up into the neck and throat. Gently move your head around in order to find the point in the centre where your head balances effortlessly on your shoulders.

5. Stand in this relaxed, centred way and again become aware of the breath. How fast/slow is it moving? What parts of your body is it flowing into and out of?

When moving into centred standing, it can help if you think of your body as being like a column of bricks stacked one on top of another, but with no cement holding them together. The column will remain upright as long as each brick is directly above the one beneath. Likewise your body will stand with minimum effort provided each part rests directly above the part beneath. When you stand in this centred way, you are using very little energy. As a result, the breath will automatically become slower and deeper. Your mind and spirit will become still.

From centred standing you may now like to move on seamlessly to the next exercise.

EXERCISE 27

Forward Bend

1. Stand in the centred way described above, becoming aware of the movement of the breath. Having given it time to become really slow, you are now ready to begin the forward bend movement.

2. At the beginning of an in-breath, bring your arms out from your sides and up above your head, holding your shoulders well back all the while. Time the movement so that your hands come together with arms straight above your head just as your lungs are completely full.

3. At the beginning of the out-breath, lean forward, bringing your out-stretched arms forward, well out from your body and towards the floor. If possible do not bend your knees or your arms. Lean forward and down until you feel a healthy stretch at the backs of your knees, legs and lower back – and no further.

4. As the breath begins to flow in again, raise your arms, holding the hands flat, palms facing upwards together in front of your body, as if you were raising something in your hands. Again try to have your arms directly overhead when the in-breath is completed.

5. With the second out-breath bring your out-stretched arms out and down, keeping your shoulders well back throughout, until your arms are back once more by your sides.

6. Repeat the sequence for as many rounds as feels comfortable.

Your knees can be 'soft' during this exercise, as it is not about trying to touch your toes without bending your knees – though this may come naturally for a few people. Try rather to enjoy the stretching sensation at the backs of your legs and lower back. Do not over-do the stretching, particularly when you are doing this for the first time. With practice you will find your body gradually becoming more flexible.

If your breath seems to be fast relative to the action, you can do the above sequence to more than two rounds of breath. For example, you might divide each upward or downward move-ment into two or more phases, and take as many rounds of breath as you need to complete the cycle. However, it is best – as a general principle – if you can move upwards (or remain still) with the in-breath; and downwards (or remain still) with the out-breath. The movements should follow and match the tempo of the breath, not vice versa. Do not intervene in any way with the breathing. Remember to allow yourself to be breathed throughout, and everything else will begin to flow naturally from that. With practice you will soon become aware of where your body is exerting itself or being stretched. Pay particular at-tention to the backs of the shoulders and upper arms, backs of legs and knees, and lower back. If you practise this exercise regularly, within a short time it will develop into a natural flowing movement that easily follows the pattern of the breath.

You can move on to develop the forward bend movement into a form of body prayer, by inserting a short prayer into the rhythm of breath and movement. The prayer is: 'O my God, I bow down before you; I offer my life to you. Amen.' It is divided into four phases in the exercise that follows.

EXERCISE 28

Body Prayer

1. While you do the forward bend, as you raise your arms, imagine that the breath is whispering or murmuring the words 'O my God'.

2. As you bend forward and down imagine the words 'I bow down before you.'

3. The words 'I offer my life to you' match the upward lifting movement with your hands in front of you.

4. The single word 'Amen' accompanies the final downward movement.

You can use your imagination as you pray with your body in this way. Lifting your arms in the third phase, see yourself offering to God something that represents you and your life. This might be the present moment, or this day, or a challenge that you face, or the work that you have to do, the food that you will prepare, the money that you own or that you will earn, or some person in your life. Then, as your hands have reached their highest point, you might imagine God receiving your gift, accepting your work, your sorrows and your joys.

You can enhance this body prayer by standing in front of a religious image or symbol, perhaps lit up by a candle or nightlight. Should you be fortunate enough to have the rising sun shining through your window as you are getting up, then the above sequence can be performed facing it. This is a good loosening-up routine as well as prayer for early in the morning. The sun marks the beginning of a new day. If, however, you have to manage without the sun, you can simply face the nearest window and let your imagination provide the sun!

The symbol of the rising sun is significant in all world religions; and it features in a passage from the gospels which is recited every day as part of the official Morning Prayer of the Church. The text is: 'By the tender mercy of our God, the dawn from on high will break upon us, to give light to those who sit in darkness and in the shadow of death, to guide our feet into the way of peace' (Luke 1:78-79). This is a reference to the anticipated birth of Jesus. But the rising sun has been particularly used as a symbol of Christ's resurrection.

Whatever time of day you do this Body Prayer, do not feel that you have to limit your use of words to those given above. You may use any word-prayer that appeals to you, though for ease of breathing, short phrases are best.

Some people find that doing body prayer like the one described above has helped them become aware of how they were unconsciously controlling the breath, and with it other issues in their lives. The realisation that there was no need to be in control then led them to becoming deeply relaxed. Praying with the body can also take you beyond a sense of yourself and your own individual concerns. One person who practised this exercise noted: 'My own preoccupations got a sense of proportion as I regarded myself as being breathed – me as part of a whole. As a matter of fact I saw how others are being breathed too, and I felt compassion and love for all creatures.'

Healing

 have been looking forward so much to this concert. Now I am sitting in the second row of the hall. The cellist and string orchestra are performing a work by John Tavener. Its execution is exquisite. And then I become aware of the tickle springing up at the top of my chest. Perhaps somebody has opened a door on this windy evening and the draught has produced in me an urgent need to cough. I try to hold it in. I cover my chest with the lapels of my jacket, pressing my hands on top of them in a desperate effort to warm and thus relax my chest. It isn't working. I will have to cough. But now I remember the breath. I imagine the in-breath as a stream of warm golden light passing through my nostrils and entering deep into my body. On the out-breath I see it flow into the itching top of my chest. After a few breath cycles, my chest feels warmer and the urge to cough is fast disappearing.

Breath is amazing. It flows in and out and carries within itself an extraordinary healing power. This has been a useful resource to get me out of embarrassing situations like the one just described. Another time was when I was travelling as a back-seat passenger on a freezing January night. The heating in the car was not great and I soon found that my feet were cold, and getting more so with every passing mile. Having nothing else to do but sit there in the numbing cold, I decided to experiment. I had noticed that my right leg was slightly colder than my left, so I attempted to make it warm using the breath. I relaxed, closed my eyes and began to focus on the breathing. On the in-breath, I imagined light and warmth filling my lungs. As the breath flowed out, I pictured a stream of warm light moving down my right leg and into my foot and toes. Continuing with this for a few minutes, I noticed that my right foot had become distinctly warmer than the left. Next, focusing on my left leg, I repeated the exercise until the left foot in turn became the warmer. Within fifteen minutes both feet were distinctly warm and remained that way until we reach our destination.

Incidents like these have taught me a valuable lesson about the healing power of the breath. They showed me that the breath, the mind and the body can work easily together to generate heat and to facilitate all-round well-being and even healing. Previously, I had thought that the breath flowed into and out of the lungs only. Now, I was discovering that the breath is able to reach into all parts of the body, irrigating them with warmth and life.

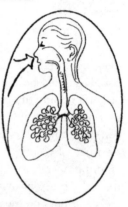

Why not try this exercise yourself next time your feet are cold?

EXERCISE 29

Foot warming

1. Sit quietly, make yourself comfortable and take some time to become aware of your body and of the contact between your body and the seat, between your feet and the floor. Slowly bring your awareness through the different parts of your body until you are satisfied that your body is quite relaxed. (Here you may like to refer back to Exercise 11 on Relaxed Sitting).

2. Become aware of the breath passing in and out. How fast or slow is it moving? Do not make the breath go fast or slow – remember you are not so much breathing as being breathed.

3. Become aware of each of your feet in turn. Which of them is the colder? Relax, close your eyes and focus on the breath once again. Bring your attention to the in-breath. As the breath comes in, imagine a stream of warm golden light flowing in through your nostrils, down the wind-pipe and filling your lungs. As the breath moves out, picture the warm golden light moving down from your chest into the side of your body where the colder foot is. See and feel the stream of warm light pass down through your leg and on towards the foot and toes, moving right out to the tips of the toes. Stay with this breath movement for about five minutes.

4. Check if this foot is now feeling less cold. You may discover that the foot which had been the colder is now warmer than the other one.

5. Do the same exercise on the other leg and foot until it in turn becomes the warmer.

Be sure to do this exercise in a relaxed, unforced way. Allow yourself to be breathed throughout and also to be warmed by the breath. Just as it is not you who are doing the breathing, neither is it you who are doing the warming. You can equally well use this exercise to bring warmth to parts of your body other than your feet, for example: your hands, head, shoulders, chest, stomach, knee or ankle.

How does breath healing work?
Bringing your awareness into a particular part of your body automatically leads to relaxation there. With the release of tension, the blood flows more easily in that area, thereby spreading warmth there. In addition, this relaxed awareness and better circulation can promote healing in injured or inflamed parts of the body.

Andrew sustained a painful injury to his left knee many years ago. Only much later did it emerge that he had ruptured a cruciate ligament. This is an injury for which many athletes nowadays are treated surgically. At the time of Andrew's injury such remedies were little talked about, and his condition is now chronic. The joint needs careful treatment. Even a slight accidental twist can cause it to become inflamed. On top of that, over the years arthritis has set in. Generally, prolonged standing or a long walk leads to some inflammation and discomfort. As a general rule, Andrew sits rather than stands whenever possible. Thus, he avoids sporting or social occasions unless there is a seat available. He also finds that in stressful situations the knee tends to 'act up'. Focusing on the breath has helped him greatly to cope with his injury. He found the healing breath exercise that follows particularly beneficial. If you are carrying a chronic injury or illness, why not try it to ease pain and stress? It works best when sitting comfortably.

EXERCISE 30

Healing breath

1. Take some time to come to a relaxed and aware sitting posture. As in the preceding exercise, slowly bring your attention to each part of your body in turn: legs, trunk, shoulders, arms, neck and throat. This awareness will automatically relax each area.

2. Focus on the breath. Do not make it go fast or slow, or flow into or out of any particular parts of your body. Remember, you do not need to breath at all. It is also important to relax your mind, letting go of any concerns about the outcome of the exercise. Being determined to get healed can create tension which may actually work against healing taking place.

3. Carry out a simple visual scan of your body to determine which part to focus on. This may not be the part that your head is telling you needs healing. Beginning at the crown of your head, slowly bring your awareness downwards through the forehead, back and sides of head, neck and throat, shoulders, chest and upper back, stomach and middle back, abdomen and lower back. Continue down through hips and legs to the toes, also shoulders and arms to the finger-tips. Where are you now feeling most tense or uncomfortable? Which part of your body is most calling for attention? Focus on this part and particularly on any pain or stress there.

4. Bring your awareness to the breath, visualising it as a stream of warm golden light both coming in and going out. On the out-breath imagine the stream of light moving towards and

into the part of your body needing healing. Let this be totally unforced. You are not pushing the breath into that area – just simply 'seeing' and feeling what is going on there.

5. Continue with the exercise for several minutes. As you stay with the process, you will notice a sense of warmth or tingling creeping into that part.

Notice that in the above exercise there is no reference to 'breathing into' the injured area, which would imply a degree of control over the healing process. Visualising or sensing the breath flowing, on the other hand, suggests that this healing breath movement is something that we receive as a gift. It is not a power that we control. Understanding that you are being breathed allows you to be relaxed throughout the exercise and more open to whatever may emerge. An attitude of trust in the healing power of the breath – or more correctly in the One who breathes through you – makes you more open to the healing process.

Some people get a straight-forward easing of symptoms through this exercise. This can happen during the meditation itself, or it may take place later. Feelings of discomfort may actually worsen for a time during the meditation, as the body clears itself. Oftentimes people get a healing other than the one they had been hoping for. One woman, whose hip had been causing her a lot of pain and discomfort, expected that it would be the area for healing. However, as she scanned her body during the exercise, her attention was drawn to her calf. Afterwards, her calf and hip both felt better. Another person came looking for a particular healing. During the meditation she let go of her desire for this, and to her surprise the breath flowed freely and deeply through her whole body.

Healing on the move
You can also practise breath healing while standing. However, it is important that you stand in as relaxed a manner as possible. Bring your attention down into both legs, and then on down into the soles of your feet. This steady awareness automatically leads to re-laxation and a centred way of standing. You will sense a lowering of your centre of gravity and a feeling of being rooted. Try to keep

your awareness within your body all the time. However, if you do find your mind wandering from time to time, remember that even intermittently bringing awareness to the breath flowing into the sick or injured part of your body will prove beneficial.

Taking the process a stage further, you may like to try practising the healing breath while walking. Physical exertion has the effect of increasing circulation and, as a result, the energy that promotes healing. Try to find a flat regular path in a quiet location the first time you try this. This will help you avoid distractions and save you from having to anticipate obstacles and surface irregularities. See this walk as a welcome break from work and other responsibilities. It is not about getting anywhere, but simply relaxing into the rhythm of the walk. Before beginning, you may like to read or re-read Exercise 24, *Walking to the breath*, in the last chapter.

EXERCISE 31

Healing walk

1. Stand at ease for a few moments. Check that you are nicely balanced between your left foot and your right, between toes and heels. Become aware of the breath – of being breathed. Do not begin the walk until the breath has become nice and slow and you have a sense of being centred.

2. Gently and slowly allow your feet to move, their movement following the movement of the breath. In a similar way to the breathing, it can feel as if you are 'being walked' rather than doing the walking. Just as there is no need to control the breath, so also now there is no need to control the walking. Do not plan how to match steps and breath. It is best to leave your mind out of the process as much as possible. Just relax and allow the breath and your feet to move in whatever way they want to. You will then discover that your feet will tend naturally to follow the breath rhythm – as happens all the time with animals and young children.

3. When the walk has been going on for several minutes, and feels natural and regular, focus on an area of your body that needs healing. Also bring your awareness to the breath, visualising it as

warm golden light as it goes in and out. On each out-breath 'see' the light smoothly flowing into the unwell part of your body.

4. Continue to observe this tranquil movement of breath and feet. Sense the flow of healing warmth. Continue the walk for at least five minutes.

5. As you conclude this exercise, take note of how the injured part of your body now feels.

Through using this exercise Andrew (mentioned earlier) found that he could undertake levels of physical activity not possible otherwise. On one occasion while holidaying he began to climb a steep mountain path. Initially his bad knee began to feel uncomfortable. He paused, taking a moment to become aware of the breath and then consciously began to walk slowly to the rhythm of the breath, centring his attention on his left knee. At the beginning of each out-breath he placed his left leg gently in front of him and moved forward. Sometimes there was just one step to the out-breath and one to the in-breath. At other times – depending on how steep the path was and how fast or slow he was going – he found himself quite naturally taking two, or even three, steps to each in-breath and out-breath. Andrew then began to see and feel the breath as a stream of warm, golden light flowing into his left knee with each out-breath. Within a short time he found the soreness easing. The leg began to feel solid and strong and he was able to continue walking without difficulty.

Coping with pain
People who suffer from chronic pain frequently discover that they are constantly tense from their efforts to fight it. Struggling to control or hold pain can be more distressing than surrendering to it. If you suffer from some painful condition, the next exercise may help you in coping with it.

Before doing this exercise you might like to read or re-read the Exercise 16, *Breath strengthening*, in Chapter Two.

EXERCISE 32

Healing triangle

1. Sit comfortably with your back upright and head well out of the shoulders. Take a few moments to slow down and become aware of being breathed.

2. Bring your awareness to the sick or injured part of your body, really experiencing the sensations, however unpleasant, in that area.

3. Tighten your fists so that the tension in your fists matches or balances the tension produced by the pain.

4. While continuing to hold this tension, bring your attention to the breath. As the breath comes in, see yourself being filled with warm golden light. With each out-breath visualise a wave of warm, golden light flowing towards the affected area.

5. As the stress in that area eases, gradually reduce the tension in your fists in tandem with it. After some time, relax completely.

6. Become aware of the distressed area. Check how it feels now.

If clenching your fists is uncomfortable, try using two soft sponge balls. Hold these lightly in your hands as you begin the exercise. Then, instead of tightening your fists, simply squeeze the sponge balls at the appropriate times.

Gillian was seriously injured in a traffic accident as a child, and had suffered much pain and post-traumatic syndrome as a result. Medical treatment successfully healed injuries to her leg and arm. She also received intensive psychotherapy, which has enabled her to move on and build a successful life. However, a twist in her neck was overlooked during treatment. The result of this has been lifelong on-going pain in her neck and sacrum. Following a quick 'scan' of her body, Gillian became aware that the area that was most calling for attention was her sacrum. Tightening her fists to match the stress in her sacrum, she visualised the breath flowing into the sacrum. This led to a noticeable easing of pain.

Subsequently Gillian told me that, while doing this exercise, she had noted a resistance to the warm energy going down through her solar plexus. She became aware of previously un-noticed tension there. As she left me, she was resolved to repeat the exercise, but this time centring on the solar plexus which was clearly calling for attention.

The healing triangle can also help in dealing with anxiety. Jacqueline, a woman in her 60s, spoke to me about her fear of speaking in public. As a young teacher, she had been constantly 'put down' due to her having a slight lisp. As a result, whenever she was due to stand and read in church, she found her heart and breath racing. During the course of her reading these symp-toms would gradually ease, but by then the reading was half over and her sense of being a failure reinforced.

I invited Jacqueline to imagine that she was due to address a conference of high-powered celebrities in five minutes time. The thought of this was sufficient to cause both her heartbeat and breath to race. I now asked her to match the resulting stress with a corresponding tightening of her fists. Then I guided her in stages to further increase the tension in her hands. This led to a progressive deepening and strengthening of her breath. I then invited her to visualise the in-breath in the form of warm golden light flowing into her body – and, as the breath flowed out, to see it as filling her whole body with warmth and light. After a few minutes of this, she was able to gradually reduce the pres-sure in her hands, while still 'seeing' the breath flowing deeply and strongly within her. I then said to Jacqueline: 'You are now strong both in breath and in spirit. You are ready and confident to go out and face your public.' Relaxed and confident, she nod-ded in agreement.

You can also use the healing triangle to cope with difficult re-lationships. Helena's son and daughter-in-law moved in with her a few years back. Relations between the two women became tense. Within a short time, Helena began to experience spasms in her shoulders and chest. Initially she feared she might be fac-ing a heart attack, which led to additional stress. Following a brief meditative scan of her body, Helena found that her shoul-ders and neck was the area of her body most calling for atten-tion. While tightening her fists to match the tension in shoulders and neck, she visualised the warm golden light of the out-breath flowing through that area. This brought about a sense of ease and peace, not just in her body, but in her spirit too.

Breath and Healing Prayer

Focusing on the breath and using your imagination can become a way of praying for healing, not just for yourself, but also for others. The next exercise is inspired by Chapter 20 of Saint John's gospel. In this text Jesus, after his death by crucifixion, suddenly appeared to his disciples. They were huddled behind closed doors, because they feared that the authorities might do to them what they had done to Jesus. Then the gospel tells us: 'Jesus came and stood among them ... He breathed on them and said to them, "Receive the Holy Spirit".' (John 20:19, 22).

You can do this meditation either sitting upright or lying flat on your back. Lying down may help to relax the breath more. Sitting up is best for dealing with distractions. Do not feel that you need to go through all the stages of the meditation at one go. Mix and match the sections in any way that seems right for you.

EXERCISE 33

Spirit breath

1. Relax and become aware of the breath as it flows in and out. Remember to always allow yourself to be breathed. Listen to the in-breath and imagine that it is whispering the words 'Holy Spirit'. Likewise imagine the out-breath whispering, 'give me your healing'. After a few rounds of breath, the complete phrase 'Holy Spirit, give me your healing' will begin to become part of you.

2. Imagine Jesus facing you, the breath moving in him to the same tempo as in you. However, the out-breath in Jesus coincides with the in-breath in you. With each in-breath, see and feel the Lord's breath as a current of warm golden light entering your nostrils and descending into your belly. Imagine that the in-breath is whispering the words 'Holy Spirit'. Stay with this movement for as long as you like.

3. Turn your attention to the out-breath and the words, 'give

me your healing'. As the breath flows out, imagine the warm golden light slowly spreading throughout your body. With each successive out-breath see the light extend further and further: up to the top of your head ..., out to your fingertips ..., down to your feet and toes. Imagine that the out-breath is whispering the words, 'give me your healing'.

4. Pay particular attention to any part of your body that may be injured or unwell. Be sensitive to any feelings of warmth, of calmness or of energy that you may find occuring in that area or elsewhere in your body.

5. Next, bring to mind any person that you love or care for, and whom you know to be in need of healing at this moment. The prayer carried on the breath now becomes, 'Holy Spirit, give N. your healing.' If you wish you might use an alternative word like 'love', 'peace' or 'joy' in place of 'healing'.

6. Picture the person you are praying for. Recall your last meeting with her, and especially her need of healing. Mentally see her in as much detail as possible. Hear her voice and, if appropriate, mentally stretch out your hand and touch her. Again become conscious of the flow of breath and the prayer phrase. Continue to allow yourself to be breathed and to hear that prayer for healing carried on the breath.

7. Picture the person slowly changing as a result of the prayer, gradually improving with each out-breath. Watch her becoming healthy in mind and body, being filled with peace and joy.

8. Broaden the scope of this prayer to include other family members, friends, neighbours or colleagues. You can apply it to groups of people as well as individuals.

This form of prayer leads to compassion. By becoming peaceful within yourself, love for others will tend to flow out without effort. Even if the person being prayed for is one whom you find difficult to love, or who has hurt you deeply, this meditation will help heal that hurt and make it possible to forgive and to love again. You can use this prayer for all kinds of human situations: healing for the sick; help for the poor, refugees, victims of violence; peace and reconciliation between individuals and nations; joy for the sorrowing or depressed; courage for those who are fearful or anxious.

Visualising positive changes during the meditation is a statement of hope, and expresses belief in the power of sincere prayer. Above all, it is an act of faith in God's power to make good things happen. This is not to say that the person prayed for will improve exactly as we picture her (though this might indeed happen!). We have many examples, however, of good things following on from prayer based on firm faith, as Jesus promised: 'Ask, and it will be given you; search, and you will find; knock, and the door will be opened for you.' (Matthew 7:7)

People have spoken of how helpful they found the Spirit breath exercise. Many saw it as a beautiful and meaningful way of praying for other people, of leaving aside their own concerns and joining with others. One spoke of feeling the prayer touching the person being prayed for. For some, it helped to clear negative feelings. One woman felt the golden light flowing out from her with love for someone with whom she had previously been very angry. Others spoke of a sense of peace and serenity and of being deeply aware of the love of the Holy Spirit for themselves, their family and the whole world. One meditator beautifully summed up the sense of being breathed, and of being prayed through by the Holy Spirit: 'I was not doing the breathing. There was no effort on my part. The breath and the prayer came from the Holy Spirit.'

CHAPTER 6

Resurrection

 was not there at the actual moment of my mother's death. It was an event my siblings and I had been anticipating ever since she had had a severe stroke some years previously. Nonetheless, her passing, like all deaths, came suddenly and was devastating beyond all expectations. The nurse who attended her tried to console me by telling me: 'Your mother breathed in and breathed out. Then she never breathed again.'

There is a last breath that will be given to each one of us. When we let go of it, it will not be followed by another. Witnessing the laboured breathing of a loved one on their deathbed throws us into the great mystery of living and dying. We can never foresee the exact moment. This uncertainly is beautifully captured in Thomas Hood's poem, *The Deathbed*:

> Our very hopes belied our fears,
> Our fears our hopes belied –
> We thought her dying when she slept,
> And sleeping when she died.

During the last few months of my mother's life, I had tried to reassure her by telling her that she would be going to a better place. Given her lifelong Catholic faith, I thought she would be happy to hear this. However, cutting through my empty words, she stunned me by replying: 'How do we know? No one has come back to tell us.' It seemed that the elderly ladies in that nursing home had been engaging in some serious and realistic theological discourse. We truly do not know what lies ahead of us – and that is what makes the thought of death so dreadful for many people. Shakespeare's *Hamlet* speaks for all of us:

But that the dread of something after death,
The undiscover'd country from whose bourn
No traveller returns, puzzles the will
And makes us rather bear those ills we have
Than fly to others that we know not of. (*Hamlet* III, 1)

Consciously becoming aware of and letting go of the breath in the present moment can help ease the fear of that great unknown. The converse is also true. Through an acceptance of the reality of our personal death, the breath within us will also ease.

Life as a single breath

A single breath cycle can be a symbol for an entire human life. In fact, that is exactly how the Bible describes our life: 'O Lord, what are human beings that you regard them, or mortals that you think of them? They are like a breath; their days are like a passing shadow' (Psalm 144:3-4) We can look at this breath symbol in two ways. In the first, the in-breath signifies life in its growth phase – birth, increase in size and strength, development of skills and accomplishments. The complete filling of the lungs symbolises maturity, the prime of life. After that a slow decline usually sets in, indicated here by the out-breath. This decline reaches its completion in physical death, expressed in the emptying of the lungs.

A more hope-filled way of looking at this cycle is to begin with the out-breath. Letting go of the out-breath symbolises acceptance of the fact that I am not in control of my life, that I am willing to surrender it, in the hope that I will receive in return a new and much richer life – symbolised by the surge of the in-breath.

The next exercise follows the ebb and flow of the breath. It can help you experience what this symbolises.

EXERCISE 34

Descent and ascent of the breath

1. Sit for a few moments with your back upright and head well out of the shoulders. Relax and allow yourself to be breathed for a few rounds.

2. Focus on the out-breath, and let it go completely. Remember that there is no need to do anything or to hold on to anything. Simply let go and allow the breath to flow out – all of it!

3. Pay particular attention to the short space between the end of the out-breath and the beginning of the in-breath. Again do not do anything – just allow the empty space to be for as long as it wants.

4. As the breath begins to flow back in, have the sense that you are now being filled with new life. Receive the new breath with gratitude.

5. Note what it feels like during the still moment when your lungs remain full.

6. Be aware of the breath as once more it begins to empty out and the cycle repeats itself. Continue with the sequence for at least five rounds.

By thinking of the breath cycle as starting with the out-breath, we experience breath as a process of going down and coming back up again. The out-breath becomes an expression of letting go, of surrender and of dying. The emptiness at the bottom of the cycle represents death itself. The in-flow of breath that follows stands for the growth of new life, which is fully expressed when the lungs are full at the top of the cycle. As always in meditations of this kind, it is essential not to force the breath in any way, but simply allow yourself to be breathed.

Our lives are filled with a multitude of contrasting couplets – successes and failures, hopes and disappointments, pleasure and pain, joys and sorrows. We would love to enjoy just the first of each of these pairings. That, however, is unrealistic. We live only by letting go, and by accepting many necessary losses. The cup has to be emptied before it can be filled up again. What you hold on to blocks you from receiving what is better. Listening to the breath in this exercise, can gradually bring you to an acceptance of life's total package.

Facing Death

The Christian faith holds that the last out-breath at the moment of physical death is not the end, but the gateway to the fullness of eternal life. The death and resurrection of Jesus is the key to what we hope for. Christ, though fully in control, freely chose to surrender his life for our sakes. Saint Paul tells us that Jesus 'emptied himself, taking the form of a slave, being born in human likeness. And being found in human form, he humbled himself and became obedient to the point of death – even death on a cross.' (Philippians 2:7-8) But this humiliation was not the end. Because of his surrender, 'God also highly exalted him and gave him the name that is above every name, so that at the name of Jesus every knee should bend, in heaven and on earth and under the earth, and every tongue should confess that Jesus Christ is Lord, to the glory of God the Father.' (ibid, 2:9-11)

    The practical question here is: how can we relate our personal experience to this message of faith? This will be the aim of the next exercise. Before doing it, you might spend a little time reading and reflecting on the scripture text given above. You will also be better prepared if you go through the last exercise on *Descent and ascent of the breath* once or twice.

EXERCISE 35

Being breathed with Jesus

1. Sit quietly and relaxed, keeping your awareness on the breath for a few rounds.

2. Bring your attention to the out-breath. As the breath is going out, imagine that it is whispering the word 'emptied'. Keep your awareness on the out-breath and this word for a few rounds of breath.

3. Focus on the bottom of the breath cycle, when your lungs are empty. Keep your awareness on this empty space, and 'hear' the word 'death', again for a few rounds.

4. As the breath flows in, stay with the word 'exalted', again for a few rounds.

5. When your lungs are full, at the top of the breath cycle, stay likewise with the word 'Lord'.

6. Bring the four phases together. Follow the entire breath cycle, keeping your awareness in turn on the four words, 'emptied', 'death', 'exalted' and 'Lord'. Continue for a few rounds.

This exercise is consoling, because it can strengthen your faith that physical death, however dark the experience may be, is not the reality that defines you. You can move towards an acceptance of death in whatever form it takes. As you go down – in life as in the meditation – you are not on your own: Jesus is with you. And, because he has conquered death, you can hope that you too will rise again. This simple meditation also puts you in touch with a basic truth of life: the drama of dying and rising isn't a once-off. It is happening many times daily for each one of us. We may struggle to avoid the slings and arrows that come our way. But this avoidance will not always work and can sometimes leave us worse off. On the other hand, when we freely accept what cannot be changed, and surrender to whatever pain or discomfort we meet with, we may be surprised by a deep sense of inner peace. The same is true each time we sacrifice ourself by acting unselfishly, and genuinely accept pain to help another.

Letting go in the many smaller situations in life can become a training in letting go, in acknowledging the temporary and limited nature of the controls that we try to exercise over events, things and people. Such practice in letting go can ease our terror in the face of bigger challenges. The greatest of these will be when we face physical death, the ultimate call to let go.

Choosing life

Fear of life, rather than fear of death, may be the more immediate issue for some people. This can be because of having felt unloved as children, or a history of disappointments in relationships or other undertakings. The experience of rejection or loss can be so deeply ingrained that they have difficulty receiving or trusting in good things. Why invest hope in this person, project or place if I believe that these will be painfully snatched from me just at the moment when I have begun to enjoy them and rely on them?

The exercise that follows can be a help to engaging joyfully with life in the present moment – despite anything that has happened in the past. It can draw your attention away from fears or anxieties about the future. It can help you focus on the real life that is given to you now, and that is being constantly renewed in you with every breath you receive. It is based on the account of the creation of the first man in the Book of Genesis (2:7): 'The Lord God formed man from the dust of the ground, and he breathed into his nostrils the breath of life; and the man became a living being.' A little further on in the chapter there is a description of the creation of the first woman out of one of the man's ribs. However, in this breath meditation we will read the verse quoted as applying equally to both women and men.

The ideal position for this exercise is lying on the floor. However, if you prefer, you can do it while seated.

EXERCISE 36

Creation meditation

1. Lie flat on your back, feet apart and with your arms just a little bit away from your sides. Relax and take some time to become aware of the breath, and of being breathed.

2. Bring your awareness to the out-breath, simply relaxing and letting it go completely. As you do so, imagine that your body is slowly beginning to melt into the ground. The image of a piece of butter melting on a slice of warm toast might help you here!

3. With each successive out-breath visualise yourself progressively melting, merging with and dissolving into the earth. 'See' the particles of your body separating and becoming one with the earth. Relax totally for a few moments, perhaps reflecting on the words used in the liturgy for Ash Wednesday, 'dust you are, and unto dust you will return'.

4. Shift your attention to the in-breath. Bring to mind the words, 'God breathed into her nostrils the breath of life.' Stay with this for a few rounds and, as you do, begin to visualise God breathing into your nostrils as the breath flows in. With each breath gratefully receive the breath of life that God is giving you.

5. As you stay focused on the in-breath, bring to mind the words, 'God formed woman from the dust of the ground'. At the same time imagine particles of earth starting to come together bit by bit to make up your body. Continue to picture your body being formed from the earth, and with each in-breath slowly emerging out of the ground, until eventually you are fully created.

6. Finally, as you lie there being breathed, become conscious of the life that God is giving you with each in-breath. Hold before your mind the words, 'woman became a living being'.

Be gentle with yourself as you do this meditation. Do not feel that you have to go through all the different stages at one go. As you begin the exercise, always take time to ensure that you are relaxed totally. Allow your lungs, rather than your mind, to do the praying. At the end of your meditation, once again observe the breathing. As compared with the beginning of the exercise, has it become any slower, smoother or deeper? Do you find yourself more relaxed, at peace or ready to trust? Do you feel more alive? Do you have a greater sense of the presence of a loving God?

Throughout this exercise try to have the sense not just that you are being breathed, but that it is God's breath that is breathing you. Doing it can bring you to an awareness that with every single in-breath the Creator is sustaining you and renewing your life. It can give a sense of the awesomeness, and yet of the intimate presence of the One who created you. People have spoken of how this helped them appreciate more deeply that life is a gift and that the breath is an on-going reminder that it is God who made us. In the words of one person, 'The repetition of the words "God formed woman from the dust of the ground, and breathed into her nostrils the breath of life" helped me to realise how special and precious I am.'

Dying to Live

During the years I lived in India I was often struck by how happy people were despite their material poverty. They seemed to have a more philosophical attitude in the face of death than we do in the more affluent and individualistic West. Could this be because they have less to lose and they have long accepted that fundamentally their lives are not under their control? On the subject of control, the Dominican author, Timothy Radcliffe makes a telling comment about the deep unease that characterises the affluent parts of today's world: 'I suspect that this pervasive anxiety derives from the fact that we have a culture of control. We can control so many things: fertility and birth, so much disease can be cured; we can control the forces of nature; we can mine the earth and dam the rivers. And we Westerners control most of humanity. But control is never complete. We are increasingly aware that our planet may be careering towards disaster ... We are afraid, above all, of death, which unmasks our ultimate lack of control.'[12]

Paradoxically, it is only through accepting death that we become free of our anxieties and fears around death. The rhythm of nature and of the seasons all involve an experience of dying in many different ways – and yet life goes on. As Christians we

---

12. Timothy Radcliffe OP, *Seven Last Words* (London, 2004), pp 47-48.

see death as the gateway into a new and richer life – the life that Jesus has won through his death and resurrection. As he himself puts it: 'Very truly, I tell you, unless a grain of wheat falls into the earth and dies, it remains just a single grain. But if it dies, it bears much fruit.' (John 12:24) Our physical death is part of a larger picture: earthly life – physical death – eternal life. Jesus uses the metaphor of the dying seed that produces a plentiful harvest, to illustrate the abundant life to which God is calling us.

As we begin to face the truth about death and all the letting-go that goes with it, we will come to know a deepening peace within us – even though dying means losing our body, our conscious mind, our loved ones and everything we have in this world. This graced peace is no illusion. A concrete example of entering wholeheartedly into this mysterious truth is that of a 30 year-old footballer, an outstanding athlete, who was wasting away with terminal cancer. The day before he died, his doctor asked him how he was. He was able to respond: 'I have never been so well in all my life. This last year has been my best ever'.

The following meditation on death and resurrection can help you cope with the fear of death – by looking at death in a concrete way. It is based on the text of Saint Paul: 'Do you not know that all of us who have been baptised into Christ Jesus, were baptised into his death? Therefore, we have been buried with him by baptism into death, so that, just as Christ was raised from the dead by the glory of the Father, so we too might walk in newness of life.' (Romans 6:3-4) Here Paul is reflecting the practice of the early Christian community, when baptism was done by immersion. The candidate was submerged fully in the water. The adult converts that Paul was writing to would have experienced being 'buried' in the water as if in a grave. It would have given them a vivid sense of going down into the tomb with Christ and being associated with his death. Then, coming up out the water, the newly-baptised person would have had a physical sense of being refreshed and more fully alive, just like a swimmer emerging from cold water.

The first time you approach this exercise, just read and reflect on these words of Saint Paul. Then you may might simply lie on your back for a few minutes. If you decide to go through the full exercise, you might move through the different stages of the meditation fairly quickly on your first time round. In time, when you feel ready for it, you can enter more deeply into the process. Its more challenging aspect is of course the first half, where the emphasis is on letting go, on dying and going down. Be gentle with yourself as you go through this part. Always give at least as much time and attention to the second ('rising') half of the meditation, for the truth is that death is overcome by resurrection. (see 1 Corinthians 15:54-56)

EXERCISE 37

Death and resurrection

1. Lie flat on your back and relax. Become aware of your body sensations. Allow some time for the breath to slow down. Focus on your sense of hearing, just noting the different sounds that are round about you.

2. Remind yourself that one day you will lie just like this in death. You will die just as surely as Jesus died. Yet, through faith, you can also rise like him from the dead.

3. Focus your attention on the out-breath. As the breath flows out, imagine that your body is slowly sinking into the ground. With each successive out-breath allow yourself to descend into your 'grave'. Keep in mind the words, 'we have been buried with him by baptism into death'.

4. As you let go of each breath, sense yourself inching your way downwards, until you are just beneath the ground; then one foot below..., two feet ..., and eventually six feet below. Rest there for a little while. You might imagine that you are lying in the tomb of Jesus, just like him surrendering your life to God.

5. Move your attention from the out-breath to the in-breath. As you receive the breath, bring to mind the words: 'As Christ was raised from the dead by the glory of the Father, so we too might walk in newness of life'.

6. With each in-breath begin to rise up inch by inch from the bottom of your 'grave'. Receive with gratitude and love the new life that God is giving you.

7. At the end of your upward movement, rest quietly on the ground for some time, perhaps 'hearing' a phrase like 'newness of life' or 'Christ was raised'.

Not suprisingly, some people are reluctant to do this meditation. Death is a subject that we might prefer not to be reminded of. Still less may we want to visualise and meditate on our own death and burial. And yet, it is in facing the mystery of death that we will overcome our fears. A mature acceptance of the truth about our personal death and resurrection in Christ can give us a sense of joy and a freedom to live our lives more fully in the present each day. Looking at death in this way is very different from a morbid fascination – the kind that can freeze the will to act and paralyse the capacity for worthwhile human and social involvement.

The imagination plays a particularly strong role in this meditation. After having gone through it, some people used words like 'queasy', 'morbid' or 'gothic' to describe their feelings around it. A few spoke of getting caught up in the physical details of being surrounded by worms and with clay on their faces. A less dramatic response was that of the woman who noted: 'I did not fully let go of my fears in relation to my own death, and I exercised control of my breathing during the process.' Again we see here how the breath reflects what the spirit is going through. However, despite their fears, most meditators were able to draw something positive from the exercise. Some found in it a way of remembering and being present to family members who had died.

People who have returned to this exercise a number of times have discovered in it ever-richer seams of meaning. Their initial fear of death gradually gave way to a sense of liberation. Some found that in letting go and going down they experienced not loneliness but a closeness to Jesus in his dying and rising. While all of this makes this process somewhat more palatable, this meditation on death and resurrection – like the reality itself that awaits – will always remain the ultimate challenge. When you are able to go through this meditation, while continuing to allow yourself to be breathed freely, then you have passed an important milestone. The release of the breath then indicates that you are well on the road to death acceptance. In one person's experience, 'I recognised a complete surrender of breath/life to Jesus and a lack of fear of death, because with Jesus death always leads to resurrection and eternal life.'

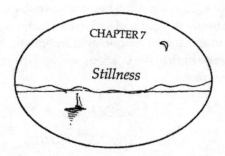

CHAPTER 7

Stillness

 t was the shortest sermon he had ever heard, and the one that had the greatest impact on him. It consisted of just two words, 'Live deliberately!' Over the years he had pondered the advice of that elderly Archbishop. They had prodded him out of complacency and comfortable routine.

People sometimes say things like, 'I always watch the nine o'clock news and weather forecast' or, 'We go to Marbella for golf in May.' For those who live deliberately there is no 'always'. 'Always' lives in the past and takes it for granted that there will be a future. In reality there is only now. Now is the only time of which we can be sure. Living deliberately means cutting down on our tendency to drift and instead living this moment to the full.

The 18th-century English writer, Samuel Johnson once said: 'When a man knows he is to be hanged in a fortnight, it concentrates his mind wonderfully'. There is surely great wisdom here. It echoes the much older wisdom of the Bible: 'teach us to count our days that we may gain a wise heart'. (Psalm 90:12)

Unconscious living fails to take on board the truth that our days are numbered. It implicitly assumes that things will continue indefinitely in much the same way as they are now – though there will be moments of fearful realisation that things don't last. The stark fact is that we only have this day and this moment to live consciously, and with a sense that it is unique and irreplaceable.

An effective way of coming into and dwelling in the present moment is simply to sit and observe the breath, without trying to control it in any way. Consciously staying with the breath can give you a sense both of the preciousness and the fragility of life in this present moment.

EXERCISE 38

Observing the breath

1. Sit quietly, taking a few moments to relax and allow yourself to be breathed.

2. Bring your attention to the in-breath. As the breath flows in, allow yourself to receive the gift of your entire life up to this point, accepting with gratitude all that God has given you over the years.

3. Shift your attention to the out-breath. Remind yourself that you will have to let go of everything you now have. With each out-breath say goodbye to something that you now have: a sum of money, an object, a place, your health, your life, a member of your family.

4. Continue with this sequence for as long as you wish. Take note of any resistance to allowing the breath to freely flow in and out.

Another breath awareness exercise is based on the very last verse from the Book of Psalms (150:6): 'Let everything that breathes praise the Lord.'

EXERCISE 39

Breath and Praise

1. Sit comfortably and relaxed, focusing on the breath.

2. As you receive and let go of the life-giving breath, listen to how it is moving in you. By virtue of this breath you are a living creature.

3. Imagine that the breath is gently murmuring the words 'praise the Lord', over and over within you. Let these words be moulded into the breath.

4. Stay with the breath and the words for at least five minutes.

In this exercise the movement of your lungs, diaphragm and chest becomes a kind of 'breath-hymn' of praise and thanks to God for the gift of the breath and of life itself.

John Main and the Prayer Word

The Irish Benedictine monk, Father John Main (1926-1982) taught a form of Christian meditation in which one internally recites a prayer word or short phrase for the entire duration of the meditation session. Before becoming a monk, John Main had lived for a time in Malaysia. There he had learned a form of *mantra* or *japa* meditation from a Hindu teacher, Swami Satyananda. Later, as a Benedictine, he traced the origin of this simple practice to Christian hermits who lived in the Egyptian desert in the third and fourth centuries. He was particularly inspired by one of these, John Cassian (365-433), who wrote about it in his *Conferences*. Main saw in the constant repetition of the same phrase a path to poverty of spirit. We become more open to God, not by filling our mind with ideas – however edifying they may be – but by allowing it to become empty. The genius of Main was in seeing that sticking relentlessly with the same 'boring' word or phrase is a most effective way to move beyond our fantasies, comforting images, desires and preoccupations – thus leaving the mind and heart more empty and open to being filled by the Spirit of God.

Under the direction of John Main's fellow Benedictine and disciple, Father Laurence Freeman, the John Main approach to meditation has spread widely, and has led to the establishment of a World Community for Christian Meditation. Thousands of groups in dozens of different countries meet weekly to meditate together. These meetings serve both to introduce people to Christian meditation and to strengthen the daily practice that Main encouraged.

The essence of John Main's Christian meditation is best explained in his own words.

EXERCISE 40

John Main meditation

1. Silently, interiorly begin to say a single word. We recommend the prayer-phrase 'Maranatha'. Recite it as four syllables of equal length.
2. Listen to it as you say it, gently but continuously. Do not think or imagine anything – spiritual or otherwise.
3. If thoughts and images come, these are distractions at the time of meditation, so keep returning to simply saying the word.
4. Meditate each morning and evening for between twenty and thirty minutes.

Many people, following Main's recommendation, use 'Maranatha' as their prayer-word. Other popular prayer phrases are 'Abba Father' and 'Holy Spirit'. 'Christians should use a Christian prayer word' – that was the instruction that Swami Satyananda gave to the young John Main. It may take some time to discover the prayer word that is right for each person. One may have to experiment with a number of these. However, it is important to persevere with one particular choice for a reasonable period of time before deciding that it is 'not working'.

Continually moving from one prayer word to another will not do justice to any one of them. In any case, irrespective of the prayer word used, the most important thing is to sit down regularly and stay with the meditation practice.

Following a meeting with John Main in 1979, I myself began using 'Maranatha' in my daily meditation. However, it's four-fold beat – or more likely my over-rigid approach to it – felt rather mechanical. When I persevered with it for about six months, I found my throat becoming increasingly sore by the end of each session. It was time to change. So, for me the prayer word since then has been 'Íosa' (pronounced 'Ee-u-sah' or more simply 'Ee-sah'). This is the Gaelic or Irish for 'Jesus'. Irish is the ancestral language of most Irish people. I was attracted to this word for a variety of reasons. Our people have been using (and continue to use) 'Íosa' in prayer for more than fifteen centuries. This name exercises a collective if unconscious force in the

spiritual lives of Irish people, including those of Irish background living abroad. Moreover, we are not accustomed to
hearing it profaned in the street. However, a particular appeal of
this prayer word is the way it so easily and naturally melts into
the breath. We will explore the connection between breath and
prayer word in the next section.

Daily Practice

If you plan to meditate on a regular basis, it is important that
you find a way to sit still for the duration of your meditation,
while at the same time being comfortable. Comfort is of the
essence. Some people are able to sit back on their heels, with or
without the help of a prayer stool or cushion. A few can manage
the lotus or half-lotus for an extended period. Such postures are
ideal. However, you should use them in meditation only if you
find them easy and natural. Sitting on a flat seat of the correct
height is equally good, provided you are relaxed, with your
body more or less forming two right-angles. This may require
adjusting the height of the seat to match the length of your legs.
If your legs are longer than the height of the seat, you can make
the seat higher by placing a folded blanket or flat cushion on top
of it. If your legs are shorter than the height of the seat, try placing the blanket or cushion on the floor underneath your feet.
After a short period of experimentation you will readily make a
seat for yourself that will help you ease into your practice.

Dress comfortably for meditation and before you begin, remove such items as shoes, watch and glasses. Before continuing
here you might like to look again at Exercise 11, *Relaxed sitting*,
in Chapter 2.

Meditating with a prayer word will be more natural if you
can mould your prayer word into the rhythm of the breath. This
will expand the meditation right down into your body – the purpose of the next exercise.

EXERCISE 41

Breath and prayer word

1. Sit comfortably. Take some time to become relaxed and aware of your body. Become aware of the movement of the breath, but without changing it in any way. How fast or slow is it? What areas of your body is it flowing into and out of.

2. Imagine that the breath in you is like a wave of the sea, coming in and going out at its own tempo. Relax into the wave of the breath, allowing it to carry you in and out without any effort on your part.

3. 'Listen' to the breath as it comes in and goes out. Imagine that it is whispering or murmuring the syllables of your prayer word.

4. Continue 'listening' to your prayer word as it, and you, are carried on the breath.

If you decide to use 'Íosa' as your prayer word, I would suggest that, as the breath is going in, 'hear' it whispering the sound 'Ee-uh' – and as it goes out, the sound 'sah'. Irrespective of the prayer word you use, this approach to prayer is passive. It is about being rather than doing. You only need to sit still and allow yourself to be breathed; and listen to the breath as it forms the prayer word for you. Then, it is not so much that you are praying as that you are being prayed through by the Holy Spirit.

Use your distractions
You will not be meditating for long before you find your mind wandering. The first kind of distraction you will encounter is physiological – you may be too warm or too cold. You may find sitting still for any length of time difficult. The exercises *Relaxed sitting* and *Breath and prayer* word should help you here. Also, I suggest that in the beginnning, short but regular periods of meditation might be sufficient. You might just start with, for example, five minutes in the morning and five in the evening. As you become more practised, you will find it easier to sit still. Then, like a seedling that has been planted, your meditation practice will tend over time to grow naturally to longer time spans.

The second kind of distraction comes from outside of you. There will be sounds that you find disturbing to your meditation. However, the real problem here is not the sound itself, but your response to it. If the phone rings when you are expecting an urgent call, or if some unexpected situation arises, you may need to discontinue your meditation right away. But occasions like these are relatively rare. The more usual external distraction is one that provokes a reaction such as: 'Those people should not be talking in here!'; 'I wish that neighbour would not use that strimmer just now!'; or 'Those boy racers are back again!' Here you have the choice between constantly rebelling against sounds like these right through your meditation, or alternately using them to help you. The latter means that each time you become aware of a sound, you accept it as a reminder that your attention has wandered outside of you. You can then calmly bring it back to the breath and to your prayer word.

Within a relatively short period of regular practice you will learn to sit still for meditation and be helped, rather than upset, by external sounds.

Going nowhere
The more persistent distractions in meditation are the ones that come from within. Your incessant internal videos and the torrent of your emotions may shock you initially. After weeks or months of practice you may be surprised and disappointed that you do not seem to be making much, if indeed any, 'progress' in overcoming these. Yet that is what the human mind is like. Indian spiritual teachers have for centuries aptly compared the mind to a large tree full of restless monkeys that constantly swing from branch to branch. Your experience might be something like this: 'Should I buy those sandals here or wait till I go to Dublin? Which train will I take? I must phone Teresa before I leave tomorrow. I am really looking forward to the holiday. It's so frustrating that my printer won't work! I must get that new anti-virus package. What is that tune that is breaking into my head just now? Did John really expect me to meet him at the station? Oh, shouldn't I be focusing on my prayer word? Where did I leave my watch: it's been missing for a whole day now? I am not looking forward to meeting with Mary next week. Did I

remember to switch off the TV properly? I've been steady on the prayer word for quite a while now – I am making progress. I wonder how long to the end of my meditation?' Your wandering mind will take you shopping, partying, on foreign holidays or to a friend's house. It will assess your 'performance' as a meditator, and much more.

The human mind abhors emptiness. It will not be satisfied with the meagre diet of just one word or phrase. The profound insights, the overlooked duties, the most seductive temptations, the deepest anxieties – as well as every kind of trivia: all of these will arise with the greatest insistence during the time of meditation. It is important to understand what is going on here. The hungry mind is desperate for the fodder of thoughts, memories, feelings and desires. However, through persevering with your prayer word, your mind will gradually become less demanding. It will begin to slow down.

As you become accustomed to inner silence, you will find yourself facing painful issues. Your mind will have you re-playing old arguments and regretting the same past action or omission over and over again. It will conjure up fears of what lies ahead of you. Repressed or forgotten hurts from the distant past will float into consciousness. These will generate waves of fresh sadness or anger at how you were treated then. But by sticking with your prayer word these issues will soften over time. As the silence of meditation gradually and gently brings them to consciousness you will be able to let them go.

Your meditation has not failed because of distractions, particularly those arising out of painful memories. No matter what comes up, be content to just keep bringing your attention back to the breath and to your prayer word. You will find yourself having to do this many times in the course of a single meditation session. Your feelings of disappointment with yourself will fade as with practice you get to know yourself better. Meditation is like a journey, but a journey that you are always beginning. It's value does not consist in feelings of relaxation or inner peace, or a totally stilled mind. What counts is being faithful, irrespective of how dry or distracted you find yourself. Bringing the wandering mind back again and again is not a digression from your meditation – it *is* the meditation. If you are distracted 30 times in the course of a single session, that means you returned to the breath and to your prayer word at least 29 times.

It means you made that number of choices to focus your attention towards God instead of on your fantasies or desirable objects. In all of this it will seem as if you are going nowhere – and this precisely is what Christian meditation is about! It is not about achieving anything, but rather about becoming detached from whatever prevents you from being pliable in God's hands.

The following 'trigger' is a simple tool that you can use to help you bring yourself back to your centre whenever you find your mind straying.

EXERCISE 42

Meditation trigger

1. Sit and become aware of your body and the movement of the breath. Allow yourself to be breathed.

2. 'Hear' your prayer word gently carried on the breath.

3. As soon as you become aware that your attention has wandered, gently touch the tips of your right thumb and index finger at the beginning of the next in-breath. At the same time bring your awareness back to your prayer word.

4. You can use this 'trigger' to draw your wandering mind back to the centre every time you become aware of being distracted.

The regular practice of meditation is a constant returning to your prayer word. As you devote time, attention and your heart to God, you will slowly and gently be moulded – spirit, mind, emotions, senses and even your body – into the person that in love you were created to be. You may not be aware of these changes taking place in your life. Those who live with you and know you best will, however, notice the difference. They will see you gradually becoming more patient and less reactive when under stress. You will be less trapped by your attachments. You will have become a more peaceful and free person.

Prayer of the Heart

The 'Jesus Prayer', also known as the 'Prayer of the Heart', dates from the earliest centuries of Christian history. However, it was little known in the West until the publication around 1925 of *The Way of a Pilgrim*. The nineteenth century Russian pilgrim who authored this book wrote about his discovery of the secret of un-interrupted prayer. As he wandered on his pilgrim route, he recited a form of the 'Jesus Prayer' in his heart many thousands of times each day. The words he used were: 'Lord Jesus Christ, Son of God, have mercy on me, a sinner.' Other ancient versions of the Jesus Prayer include, 'Jesus, Son of God, have mercy on me', or simply the name 'Jesus'. Commenting on the Jesus Prayer, the 19th-century Russian Orthodox saint, Theophan the Recluse (1815-1894) recommends that, while praying it, one should bring one's attention into the heart: 'In order to keep the mind on one thing by means of a short prayer, it is necessary to preserve attention and so lead it into the heart; for so long as the mind remains in the head, where thoughts jostle one another, it has no time to concentrate on one thing. But when attention descends into the heart, it attracts all the powers of the soul and body into one point there.'[13]

Bringing your attention into the heart means focusing on the heart centre. This is not the heart organ itself, but the small zone in the centre of the chest towards which you instinctively point when you say 'me'. This 'me' centre becomes the focus of atten-tion in the 'prayer of the heart'. In this form of prayer you keep your attention on your prayer word within the heart (or 'me') centre. Then you will discover a new sensation in this centre. As Theophan puts it: 'This concentration of all human life in one place is immediately reflected in the heart by a special sensation that is the beginning of future warmth.'[14] Paying attention to the varying moods of this sensation will help you bring your aware-ness out of your head and into your body. It will also facilitate perseverance with your prayer word.

The exercise that follows puts the above into practice. However, it has an additional feature in that it also focuses on the breath as it moves through the heart centre.

13. *The Art of Prayer, an Orthodox Anthology*, compiled by Igumen Charlton of Valamo (London 1966), p 94.
14. Ibid.

EXERCISE 43

Prayer word, breath and heart centre

1. Sit comfortably with your back upright. Become aware of your body and of being breathed.

2. Bring your awareness to your heart centre, that small zone in the centre of your chest that you instinctively point to when you say 'me'.

3. Become aware of the sensations in the heart centre. What word might you use to describe them: 'soft', 'hard', 'warm', 'cold', 'tender', 'ticklish', or what?

4. Notice how the breath, as it comes in and goes out, always passes through the heart centre. As it does so, take note of any changes of feeling in the heart centre. What word would best describe the new feeling?

5. Keep your awareness on the breath as it flows through the heart centre. Hear it gently murmur your prayer word.

6. For the remainder of your meditation just keep your awareness within the heart centre, on the flowing breath there, and on your prayer word.

7. Each time you find your mind wandering, gently bring it back to the heart centre, the breath and the prayer word – again and again, right to the end of your meditation.

Those who practise this exercise find that they are less prone to being distracted. It tends to bring about a sense of peace and joy in the heart. As one person put it: 'I had been feeling a heaviness in my centre and focusing on it during that exercise really helped me'

The more you practice meditation with your prayer word, the more it will become part of you. Your word will arise in your consciousness, not just at the times of meditation, but at quiet moments during the day. At times of intense busy-ness and pressure you can turn to it as an antidote to information overload. As you continue to meditate faithfully with your prayer word, the word will be your constant companion and friend. You will begin to have the sense that it is not so much that you are carrying it, but that it is the prayer word, or rather, the One you invoke through the prayer word, who carries you.

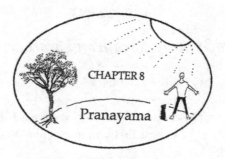

CHAPTER 8

Pranayama

he Sanskrit term *pranayama* is derived from *prana* ('life force') and *yama* ('restraint'). It refers to specific yoga exercises designed to control the flow of the breath. Through pranayama the breath can be made to run deeper and more smoothly, and at different tempos. It can also be directed into and out of specific parts of the body. Many practitioners use pranayama to improve their health. However, in the Indian yoga context within which pranayama evolved, it has primarily been a means of preparing the body for prolonged and deep meditation.

One might well ask: how does the use of pranayama relate to the practice of 'allowing the breath' as described in this book? Or indeed, can the two be reconciled at all? In response, we can say that where the breath is concerned, gentleness and patience is paramount. It is not something that we own and can manipulate, but rather a mystery that we must respect. A reflection of this is the fact that in India reputable yoga teachers will teach pranayama only after they have satisfied themselves that the candidate is ready for it. This presupposes at least that a person has reached the stage of being able to allow the breath to flow freely in them – that he or she is able to be aware of the relaxed movement of the breath, without succumbing to the need to take control of it. Once this is the case, many benefits can flow from pranayama, including deeper relaxation and enhanced energy.

There are, however, some people for whom pranayama is not advisable. These include those whose nervous system has been damaged through drug or alcohol abuse, or who suffer from certain forms of mental illness. People affected by asthma or shortness of breath should avoid pranayama exercises until these ailments have been brought under control. In the meantime they should confine themselves to passive breathing exercises like those described here in earlier chapters. To be able to relax and allow oneself to be breathed is already a huge step forward. It is sadly one that many in today's highly pressured world are unable to take.

The Practice

If you feel drawn to practise pranayama, I recommend that you consult a competent guide in the practice – that is, if you are fortunate enough to find one. If you do decide to try it on your own, the important thing to remember is that you are never fully in control of the breath. The notion of control implies that you decide 'to breathe', that you select the tempo and also those parts of your body into which the breath will run and out of which it will flow. The reality however, is that before you ever 'take control', the breath has already for many years been moving within you in its own way. Taking control of the breath in a way that does not respect the pre-existing rhythm is counter-productive. The outcome may well lead to symptoms such as headaches, dizziness, sore throat, or tension in the stomach and abdominal areas. It may in some cases bring about a kind of 'high' that has some parallels with the effects of alcohol or drugs.

People who have undertaken yoga training may be familiar with 'fast breathing' techniques such as *kapalabhati* ('that which brings lightness to the skull'); and *bastrika* ('bellows') breath, which is highly energising. *Ujjayi* ('victorious') breathing involves producing a snoring or hissing sound in the throat, and can relieve hypertension and anxiety. *Bhramari* means literally 'big black bee'. It is believed to relieve throat ailments. It is beyond our scope here to examine these and other more advanced practices.

The simplest pranayama exercises are single and alternate nostril breathing. You can try these provided both of your nostrils are not blocked. Before attempting them check that you are sitting upright (see, for example, the Exercise 11, *Relaxed sitting* in Chapter 2). For both of these practices you use the fingers of the right hand to block the nostrils. Fold the index and middle finger of your right hand in towards the palm. Then you can use the thumb for blocking the right nostril and the ring and little fingers for blocking the left.

EXERCISE 44:

Single nostril breathing

1. Become aware of your body and allow yourself to be breathed for several minutes.

2. At the beginning of an in-breath use your right thumb to block the right nostril, thus allowing the breath to pass in and out through the left nostril only.

3. After a few rounds of breath, lower your arm and allow yourself to be breathed through both nostrils, again for a few breaths.

4. Block the left nostril with the ring and little fingers of your right hand, allowing the breath to flow only through the right nostril, for the same number of breaths.

5. Lower your arm and allow yourself to be breathed through both nostrils.

On your first day of practice do just one round of breath on each side. Then you can add a breath each subsequent day until you reach a number that is comfortable for you. Unless you have a guide, I recommend that you limit yourself to five or at most ten breaths on each side.

You can use the same hand position for closing the nostrils in doing alternate nostril breathing.

EXERCISE 45

Alternate nostril breathing

1. Become aware of your body, allowing yourself to be breathed for several rounds.

2. At the beginning of an in-breath, close the right nostril with your right thumb, thus causing the air to move in through the left nostril only.

3. When the lungs are full, close both nostrils momentarily. Then, as the breath goes out, open the right nostril while keeping the left nostril closed. This causes the breath to flow out through the right nostril only.

4. Allow the breath to flow back in through the right nostril.

5. Again briefly close both nostrils briefly before allowing the breath to flow out through the left nostril.

6. This completes one cycle of alternate nostril breathing.

On your first day do just one round of alternate nostril breathing. If you wish you can gradually add an extra round on subsequent days – up to a number that seems appropriate to you. The maximum again should be between five and ten, unless you are being guided. At the beginning and end of each practice always sit quietly, simply being breathed for three or four rounds. This ensures that you are relaxed, with the breath nice and slow, before you start and after you conclude single or alternate nostril breathing

When you practise in the way described here, you are still allowing yourself to be breathed. The breath continues to flow at its own tempo, not one determined by you. At no time do you actively inhale or exhale. Apart from placing the thumb and fingers on the nostrils, the flow of breath remains passive in every other respect.

With gentle practice over time, you can integrate these pranayama exercises into the practice of meditation with a prayer word. This will cause the breath – and your meditation – to flow more deeply and smoothly.

Before doing the following, you might like to re-visit Exercise 41, *Breath and prayer word* in Chapter 7.

EXERCISE 46

Pranayama and prayer word

1. Sit still, becoming aware of your body and of being breathed for at least a few rounds of breath.

2. Gently begin single or alternate nostril breathing.

3. As you focus on the breath moving in and out through a nostril, imagine that it is whispering your prayer word.

4. Continue with your pranayama only for as long as feels comfortable – typically up to five or six rounds. Then, gently lower your arm.

5. Continue with your meditation as usual, keeping your awareness on the breath and on your prayer word.

APPENDIX A

The Renaissance and Descartes

The Renaissance usually refers to a cultural shift which had its beginnings in 15th-century Italy. The focus of attention in architecture, art, music and writing gradually started moving from God to man. Its chief protagonists coined the term *'rinascimento'* (Italian) or *'renaissance'* (French), which literally mean 're-birth', because they believed that much of the wisdom of the ancient world, which had been lost to Europe during earlier centuries, was now being re-discovered. A culture was being born, involving new ways of thinking in every field of human endeavour. The Renaissance was followed by other important developments in European history such as the Reformation and the discovery of new continents. Most significantly, it triggered the development of the empirical sciences which really took off in the 16th and 17th centuries and were crucial in the formation of the modern era.

Few Renaissance figures have had as great an influence on today's world as the French philosopher Rene Descartes (1596-1650). His thought combined doctrines about God taken from great Christian thinkers such as Augustine, Anselm and Aquinas, with a critical methodology taken indirectly from the Skeptic philosophers Pyrrho and Sextus Empiricus. He also carried out many physical and anatomical experiments. For example, in optics he discovered the law of refraction, and in meteorology he explained the rainbow. He was also one of the greatest mathematicians of the age, and invented analytic or co-ordinate geometry.

Descartes' most important contribution to western culture was his re-modelling of philosophy on mathematical principles. Mathematics is the clearest of all the sciences and Descartes strove to bring mathematical-like clarity and unquestionable certainty to our understanding of the human person and of God.

In his most important work, *Discourse on Method* (1637), he developed his method of universal doubt. He started from the position that everything was to be considered uncertain unless or until it could be established from self-evident propositions. After much reflection he came to just one truth of which he could have no doubt. This was the reality of his own existence, which was absolutely certain. If he did not exist, he could not be thinking as he was right then. He summed up this conclusion in his now famous saying, *'cogito, ergo sum'* or *'je pense, donc je suis'* ('I think, therefore I am'). He went on to conclude: 'From that I knew that I was a substance, the whole essence or nature of which is to think, and that for its existence there is no need of any place, nor does it depend on any material thing; so that this "me", that is to say, the soul by which I am what I am, is entirely distinct from body, and is even more easy to know than is the latter; and even if the body were not, the soul would not cease to be what it is.'[15] From this founding principle he was able to arrive at other truths which he could likewise hold as being certain. These include the existence of God and the immortality of the soul.

Descartes' method provided a philosophical context for the explosion of mathematical and scientific discoveries that were to be made in the years and centuries that followed. However, there was a downside. In declaring that thinking was the true nature of the human person, Descartes implied that the body is not part of who one is. This alienation of the human person from his/her body was just part of a general split between mind and spirit on the one hand – and a machine-like material world on the other.

Descartes' method of universal doubt put much that had been accepted without question up to that time into a secondary position. In particular, it undermined theological speculation and religious doctrine by implying that most of their conclusions were 'uncertain'. He himself remained a man of faith and continued to practise his Catholicism, which had been underpinned through his education by the Jesuits. However, later generations of thinkers would embrace his philosophy without sharing his faith. Even before Descartes' time a divide between

15. R. Descartes (1637). *The Philosophical Works of Descartes*, rendered into English by Elizabeth S. Haldane and G. R. T. Ross, vol 1, p 101. NY: Cambridge University Press (1970), p 249.

religion and secular learning had started opening up in western thought. His philosophy of clear and distinct ideas widened that gap by giving it a philosophical basis. This dualism exists on a number of levels as illustrated by two sets of ideas, represented here in columns, that would now be widely perceived as opposing one another:

GOD	WORLD
MIND	MATTER
SPIRIT	BODY
FAITH	FACT
THEOLOGY	SCIENCE
RELIGION	TECHNOLOGY

The words in the left hand column represent concepts that have their roots in the medieval world and earlier, many of which cannot be grasped directly by the senses. Their cultural expression is still to be seen in great cathedrals and in the philosophy, art, music and literature of those centuries. The supreme science in this worldview is theology, which puts God at the top of its value system. The names in the right hand column refer to material things that can be observed, measured and utilised. Scientific investigation had been going on for many centuries before Descartes' time, but it was always seen as part of philosophy and in total harmony with, if not subservient to, theology. Henceforth it would develop independently, first of theology and eventually too of philosophy. Scientific discoveries would give rise to the technologies that power our civilisation. Truth would come to be seen more and more as that which could be verified scientifically, or which led to positive practical results. We see the outcome of this technological revolution in every aspect of life today: modern industry, transport, nuclear energy, bio-technology, communications, the internet and the world of medicine.

APPENDIX B

Breath and Spirit in Ancient Languages

Prior to the seventeenth century in Europe, and later elsewhere, people made little if any distinction between the physiological breath and the human spirit in each individual. This becomes clear when we look at the key terms for breath and spirit in Hebrew, Greek and Latin, the ancient languages through which European culture was formed. The same is true when we look at the corresponding terms in Sanskrit and Mandarin Chinese, which played a similar role in the cultures of India and China.

The Hindu scriptures were for the most part written in Sanskrit. It is a language which is still used today by philosophers and spiritual teachers. The Sanskrit term *prana* can mean either 'breath', 'wind', 'life' or occasionally 'the Supreme Spirit'. However, the more usual term for the Supreme or Univeral Spirit is *atman*, which too can mean 'breath', 'soul' or 'self' in a general sense. *Prana* is particularly identified with the 'life-force', the vitality that keeps a person alive, or it can mean simply 'life'. It is, however, most commonly used in reference to the breath. *Pranayama* means the 'control' (*yama*) of the 'breath' (*prana*), by means of breathing exercises. Yoga practitioners use pranayama to bring about calmness, emotional stability, inner clarity and a ability to centre the attention. This in turn paves the way for the discipline of meditation. Diet and a clean environment are important requirements for the successful practice of pranayama.

The corresponding term for breath or spirit in classical Chinese is *chi* (as in *t'ai chi*), also written as *qi* (as in *qigong* – pronounced *'chi kung'*). *T'ai chi* is a form of exercise, best known for the graceful flowing movements and poses of its practitioners. *Qigong* is a way of managing the breath to achieve and maintain good health and energy. *Qi/chi* can mean 'breath', but also the vital 'force' or 'spirit' that animates the human body. Practices such as *t'ai chi* and *qigong* are aimed at enhancing health and spiritual power.

The same kind of overlap between breath and spirit is evident also in Latin. Here *spiritus* can mean 'breath', 'breathing' or 'air', but also 'soul' or 'life'. *Anima* can signify 'breathing', 'wind', 'breeze' or 'air' – but also 'soul', 'spirit', 'vital principle' or 'life'. What is striking about both of these Latin words is how, just like the corresponding terms in the eastern cultures, *spiritus* and *anima* can both stand either for the concrete 'breath' or the more ethereal 'spirit'.

The terms used in Hebrew and Greek are of particular relevance for Christians, because these respectively were the languages in which the Old and New Testaments were written. What then does scripture tell us about the 'breath' and 'spirit'?

Breath and Spirit in the Old Testament

There are two words in the Hebrew Old Testament that correspond to the English word 'breath'. These are *ruach* and *neshmath*. *Ruach* occurs almost 400 times. It can mean a range of things including 'air', 'breeze', 'wind', 'breath', 'mind', 'soul' or 'spirit'. It is used for the Spirit of God that 'hovered over the water' (Gen 1:2). The more earth-bound term *neshmath* is used only twice. It can mean 'breath', 'wind', 'life' or even 'a human being'. Its most important occurrence is in Gen 2:7: 'The Lord God formed man from the dust of the ground, and breathed into his nostrils the breath (*neshmath*) of life; and the man became a living being.' However, unlike *ruach*, *neshmath* never corresponds to the English 'spirit'.

God lends us the breath (*ruach*) for the duration of our earthly life, but all the time it remains God's breath. We are alive because God breathes in us and thus animates us. When we die, our body returns to the earth, but the *ruach* returns to God: 'When you take away their breath (*ruach*), they die and return to their dust. When you send forth your spirit (*ruach*), they are created; and you renew the face of the ground.' (Ps 104:29-30). This dependence on God's gift of breath or spirit applies to all living beings (see also Job 34:14-15). Giving up one's spirit to God is the same as surrendering one's final breath: 'Into your hand I commit my spirit' (Ps 31:5). The word for 'spirit' here is *ruach*, so the verse can equally well be written: 'Into your hand I commit my breath.'

In the third and second centuries BC a Greek translation of
the Hebrew Old Testament was made by a team of seventy
Jewish scholars. It has been called the Septuagint – *septuaginta*
being the Latin for 'seventy'. This Old Testament Greek text was
much used by the early Christian community.

Breath and Spirit in the New Testament
Following on the Septuagint, the Greek New Testament translated
the Hebrew *ruach* as *pneuma*. *Pneuma*, like *ruach*, has the same
multiple meanings. It can be 'air', 'breath', 'wind', as well as
'spirit'. The verb corresponding to *pneuma* is *pneo*, which means
'to blow' or 'to breathe'.

The conversation between Jesus and Nicodemus in John 3 is
particularly revealing of the different meanings of *pneuma* in the
New Testament. Here Jesus teaches that one can enter the kingdom of heaven only through being born from above 'of water
and the Holy Spirit (*ek hudatos kai pneumatos*)' (John 3:5). Verse 8
has Jesus declaring: 'The wind blows wherever it chooses (*to
pneuma hopo thelo pnei*), and you hear the sound of it, but you do
not know where it comes from or where it goes. So it is with
everyone who is born of the Spirit' (John 3:8). The force of this
line cannot be fully appreciated in English or in modern languages generally, where the words for 'wind' and 'spirit' are unrelated. In the original Greek both are rendered by *pneuma*.
What God's Spirit and the wind have in common is not just that
it is impossible to predict in exactly what ways they will move.
They also share the same name.

At the Last Supper Jesus promises his disciples another
Counsellor: the Spirit of truth (John 14:16-17). This Spirit comes
upon the apostles at Pentecost in the form of a powerful wind.
Here the word for wind is *pnoe*, closely related to *pneuma* (Acts
2.2). As well as in the form of wind, here the Holy Spirit mani-
fests in the form of fire. Both of these images, plus a third one,
that of water, are used throughout the scriptures to express the
mobility and the unpredictability of the actions of God's Spirit.

At his death Jesus surrenders his Spirit back to God: 'Father,
into your hands I commend my spirit (*pneuma*).' (Luke 23:46)
Because *pneuma* has the same duality of meaning as the Hebrew
ruach, the last prayer of Jesus can equally well be written in

English: 'Father, into your hands I commend my breath.' And as the gospel points out in the very next sentence, that is just what Jesus did: 'Having said this, he breathed his last.' In the Greek text of this sentence, the word 'breathed' (*exepneusen*) is derived from *pneuma*. It means literally 'he breathed out his *pneuma*'.

On the evening of Easter Sunday, the risen Jesus appeared to the disciples who were fearfully huddled behind closed doors. In the course of that meeting Jesus 'breathed on them' and said: 'Receive the Holy Spirit.' The word for 'breathed' here is *enephusesen*, past tense of *emphusao* ('to breathe into', 'in' or 'upon'). This word is used only once in the Septuagint Greek translation of the Old Testament, and that is in Gen 2:7 where God breathed on Adam and he became a living being. It is clear that John is continuing where Genesis left off. Just as the original gift of human life was through being in-breathed by God's Spirit, so also the gift of eternal life through Christ's resurrection comes about through a new in-breathing of that same Spirit, this time given by the risen Jesus himself.

If you want to know more ...

The questions that follow are a representative sample of those that people have most frequently asked during courses in meditation over the years. They fall under four headings.

A. Practicalities of breathing

Q. Which is correct – to breathe through the mouth or through the nose?

A. Do not breathe at all! Allow the breath to move as it will. Left to itself, the breath will tend to move in and out through the nose all the time. However, it you are suffering from a cold or are carrying a nasal injury, one or both nostrils may have become blocked, thus preventing full nasal breathing, at least for a time.

Q. When I practise my yoga exercises I breathe slowly in through the nose and out through the mouth. Is this correct?

A. The deeper question here is: who is doing the breathing? Is breathing something you need to do, and in a specific way – or, can you just let it happen? When you allow yourself to be breathed, then you do not need to be concerned about how fast/slow, through the nose/mouth or into/out of which parts of your body the breath is flowing.

Q. My psychotherapist occasionally urges me 'breathe out' when I am distressed. How do I reconcile that with 'being breathed'?

A. The psychotherapist's recommendation is sound advice for most people. When you are distressed is not the time for learning a new technique. However, as you become more practised in allowing the breath, then you will be able quite naturally to focus on 'being breathed', even when under stress.

Q. Can awareness of the breath help me to sleep?

A. Focusing on the breath brings your awareness away from the mind and down into your body. As you stay with the breath – particularly if you use a prayer word with it – you will leave behind you the things that give you sleepless nights. (See also Exercise 6 in Chaper 1, *Breathing to sleep*).

Q. When I become aware of my breathing, I find that instead of slowing down, it gets faster. Why is this?

A. Experiencing the relaxed breath for the first time, can for some people seem scary. They may feel a kind of need to do something. This can lead to tension, which in turn can cause a speeding up of the breath. However, by gently bringing one's awareness back just to the breath, the breath will after a while automatically become slower, smoother and deeper.

Q. As I try to relax my breath I realise there is a block at the top of my chest.

A. Relaxing is effortless, the opposite of trying. Simply bring your awareness to what is actually going on in your body. The relaxation will happen by itself. A block or tension in some area of your body may be an indication of something you are holding on to. Gently bringing your awareness to that tense area may in time reveal just what the issue is.

Q. I find the idea of being breathed quite threatening, like being deprived of the right to manage an intimate part of my life. In the beginning it seemed such an innocuous idea. Now I realise that it is challenging me re all the things I do not want to let go of.

A. All of this is because of the intimate union between breath and spirit in each one of us. In facing the breath, you are facing all of your life issues – including the challenges. Hopefully the exercises in this book will help you with these.

B. The Prayer Word and Distractions

Q. How do I decide on a prayer word for meditation?

A. John Main's teacher, Swami Satyananda encouraged him, a Christian, to use a Christian prayer word. Main adopted the word 'Maranatha'. Select from your own prayer tradition a word or short phrase that 'feels' right for you and stay with it for several weeks at least. With regular practice, you will in time be drawn to the right prayer word for you – which may or may not be the one you started out with.

Q. How often and for how long should I meditate?

A. In the beginning you might stay at it for as little as five minutes once or twice a day. If you persevere with this, you will find your-self wanting more. The time you spend will gradually lengthen and your meditation will deepen. Two half-hour periods daily would be ideal.

Q. Do I need to be aware of the breath and the prayer word during meditation – or just the prayer word?
A. First become aware of the breath and being breathed. Then imagine that the breath is gently murmuring your prayer word.

Q. I have a very short meditation word – almost one syllable. My breath in and out is much longer. Do I keep one word per breath in and one word per breath out, or have several words per breath?
A. Just sit and take time to become aware of the breath. Allow yourself to be breathed, and then 'listen' to the flow of the breath. There is nothing you need do, except 'hear' the breath murmur or whisper the prayer word. That, rather than your mind, will determine whether you will have one or several words per breath.

Q. I get very easily distracted during the time of meditation, with a million things running through my head at the same time. What should I do?
A. Distracting thoughts are inescapable, but they can become your ally. Every time during your meditation that you become aware of losing the focus, simply bring your attention back to the breath and your prayer word and resume. Having 30 distractions of this kind is better than one or two, because it means that you are making a real act of faith at least 29 times – sacrificing your fantasies, thoughts, even your 'brilliant' insights in order to be available to the Holy Spirit.

C. Meditation and Christianity

Q. All this relaxing and 'allowing the breath' is very nice. But is it prayer?
A. Practising body awareness or allowing oneself to be breathed are not prayer in themselves – but then neither is the recitation of prayers, or even reading a passage of scripture. Real prayer involves opening up your heart and surrendering yourself to God and his loving plans for you. If 'allowing the breath' leads you deeper into this kind of relationship with God, then it is certainly prayer.

Q. Can meditation be selfish or escapist?
A. You will find the answer by reflecting on the following questions: Are you neglecting responsibilities to family and others because of the time you give to meditation? Do you see meditation as a refuge from the challenges of life, a way of closing your eyes to what God is really asking of you? Do you meditate to get pleasant experiences? Do you meditate just to develop your mental powers? Is meditation making you more self-centred and less concerned with the well-being of others?

Q. What do you say to people who insist you cannot incorporate centring techniques or anything related to yoga and Eastern religions into prayer and still call it Christian?
A. Some eastern and New Age practices can cause a person to become more open to beliefs that are alien to Christianity, for example, reincarnation or occult 'spirit guides'. However, there are simple practices involving the body, the imagination and the breath that are used in yoga but that have for centuries also been used in other religious contexts, including Christian. These are God's gifts and can certainly be used in Christian prayer.

Q. What makes meditation Christian?
A. Christian meditation is not primarily about relaxation or inner peace, though it certainly does not exclude these. Nor is it about getting a 'high' or anything else for yourself. Christian meditation is about giving yourself to God in Jesus Christ, to experience something of his death and resurrection even as you meditate. This will come about as you continually re-focus your attention each time it wanders from the prayer word. Over time, this will hollow out a space in your heart that will allow the risen Lord to enter deep within you.

D. The effects of Meditation
Q. What are the long-term benefits of meditation?
A. After an initial period during which you find meditation physically and mentally relaxing, distractions will grow as you start getting 'bored' at staying with just the same prayer word. Here your mind is reacting to no longer being the centre of attention. It will reach for any kind of distracting mental fodder.

However, if you continue returning to your prayer word, your life will slowly be transformed. You may not notice the change, but those round about you will – as you become more tolerant, less reactive and easier to live with.

Q. I have just started to practise Christian meditation with a prayer word. However, I find a pain building up in my chest and have had to discontinue.
A. If you are getting mildly negative sensations, it is best to focus your awareness on these as you meditate. Staying with the sensation itself will over time help you gain insight into where it is coming from. If meditation is causing you to experience pain, you do need to go gently, and only for short periods of time. The physiological reaction as you meditate may be the result of an unhappy experience associated with meditation in the past. As you gently face whatever the issue may be, the symptoms will lose their energy.

Q. Is it possible to have too much meditation?
A. Two hours daily should be regarded as the maximum, unless you are an experienced meditator or are practising under a competent spiritual director. Too much meditation, especially for a beginner, runs the risk of leading to hallucinations, impairment of the ability to relate to other people and a general inability to cope with the practical demands of life.

Q. What about hallucinations, visions and psychic phenomena?
A. Strange sensations, inner lights and sounds, feelings – both sweet and unpleasant – can occasionally occur during meditation. Do not take too much notice of them. They may simply be your senses and emotions craving attention. Just continue with your meditation, focusing on your prayer word. Usually these effects will fade away by themselves.

If, however, you experience repeated frightening 'presences', then you should seek competent spiritual advice. Such phenomena can for some people be the residue of drug or alcohol abuse, or of earlier negative spiritual experiences, involving ouija boards, seances or other psychic activities.